THE
SPIRITUAL
TEACHINGS
OF
MARCUS
AURELIUS

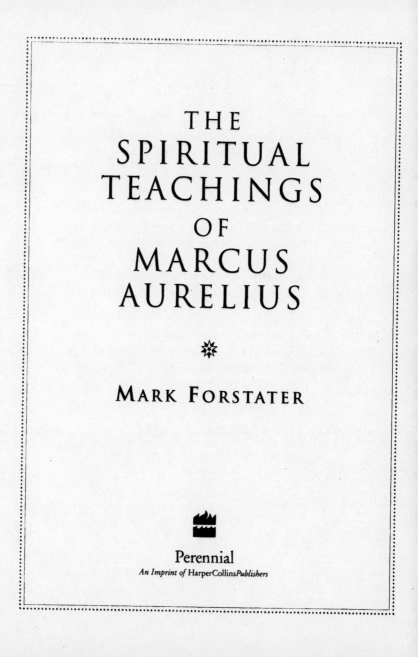

THE
SPIRITUAL
TEACHINGS
OF
MARCUS
AURELIUS

❋

MARK FORSTATER

Perennial

An Imprint of HarperCollins*Publishers*

A hardcover edition of this book was published
in 2000 by HarperCollins Publishers.

THE SPIRITUAL TEACHINGS OF MARCUS AURELIUS.
Copyright © 2000 by Mark Forstater.

HarperCollins books may be purchased for educational,
business, or sales promotional use.
For information please write: Special Markets Department,
HarperCollins Publishers Inc., 10 East 53rd Street, New
York, NY 10022.

First Perennial edition published 2001.

Designed by Nancy B. Field

Library of Congress Cataloging-in-Publication Data
is available.

ISBN 0-06-095510-4

08 09 ❖/RRD 10 9 8

To Paul, who read him;
To the women in my life,
and especially to Jo,
who showed me the way.

There will come a time when I will send a famine in the land, not a famine of bread or a drought of water, but a famine of truth.

—Amos 8:11

The life of the dead rests in the remembrance of the living.

—Cicero

CONTENTS

❖

ACKNOWLEDGMENTS

❀

The author would like to thank the following people for helping in the creation of this book and audiotape:

Robert Gwyn Palmer for some sagely advice.

Rupert Lancaster of Hodder Audiobooks for commissioning the audio production.

My assistant Sian Buckley for her help in selecting, editing, typing, naming, and making suggestions for the text, and generally supporting me through the writing process. Danielle Evenson for typing and assisting.

My editors Rowena Webb at Hodder & Stoughton and Marjorie Braman at HarperCollins, who had faith in the project.

Professor Chris Clarke of the University of Southampton for checking my dodgy science.

Professor Richard Sorabji of Kings College,

London, for discussions on the Stoics and in particular for bringing my attention to Jim Stockdale.

The many friends who read early drafts and gave valuable suggestions.

Derek Jacobi for a very fine reading of the texts.

My agent, Liv Blumer, who had the vision and expertise to turn an interesting idea into a viable book.

And finally, my wife, Jo, who had to live for many months with two Marcuses in the house, when one was more than enough.

PREFACE

❉

Marcus Aurelius was a Roman emperor and a philosopher. In his own estimation, living life as a philosopher was more important than ruling the most powerful empire of his time. He practiced his philosophy daily so that he could command the empire without losing his treasured ideals of justice and humanity.

The philosophy that he lived by is one of empowerment, independence, and self-reliance. Its principles led him to a life of spiritual contentment as well as worldly attainment, a potent combination that most people still find impossible to achieve.

Marcus Aurelius wrote a book of "spiritual exercises" for himself that was in effect the first self-help book ever written. Now, nearly two thousand years after it was composed, we can put these selfsame principles into practice at home, at work, with friends, relatives, and strangers. Remarkably, his philosophy is still accessible and relevant to our twenty-first century lives.

———•———

Part One of this book is an introduction to Marcus Aurelius, his life and his philosophy. It explains how this book came to be written and how it is organized. Part Two contains the actual spiritual exercises, grouped into eight chapters.

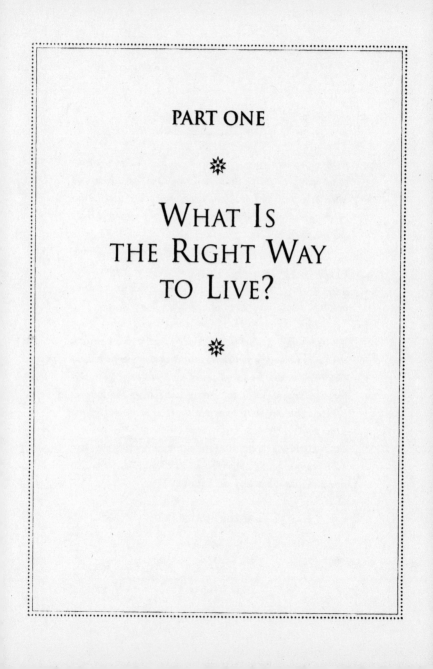

PART ONE

❋

WHAT IS THE RIGHT WAY TO LIVE?

❋

Remember that even if you were to live for three thousand years, or thirty thousand, you could not lose any other life than the one you have, and there will be no other life after it. So the longest and the shortest lives are the same.

For this present moment is shared by all living creatures, but the time that is past is gone forever. No one can lose the past or the future, for if they don't belong to you, how can they be taken from you?

Keep in mind these two things: First, that since the beginning of time the cycles of creation have shown the same recurring patterns, so it makes no difference if you live for one hundred years, two hundred years, or forever. Second, that the person who lives the longest life and the one who lives the shortest lose exactly the same thing.

For the present moment is the only thing you can take from anyone, since this is all they really own. No one can lose what they do not own.

—MARCUS AURELIUS

I'm sitting in a cybercafé in Soho, London, sipping on a cappuccino.

Inside, young business men and women with mobile phones keep in touch with their offices, friends, and lovers across the country. Travelers sit at consoles surfing the Internet and collecting e-mail from around the world.

Outside, cars, taxis, and buses crisscross the polluted city ferrying people through the crowded streets. Below my feet, underground trains speed through the bowels of the earth. Nearby, high-speed trains depart for Brussels, Paris, and Rome.

Overhead, planes with hundreds of people on board travel vast distances. Unseen, communication satellites circle the earth.

Although we live in a time of an incredible explosion in communications, knowledge, and wealth, we have begun to realize that it will not be possible to sustain the life we are currently leading for very much longer.

We are faced with a world that is suffering at our own hands. Science, technology, and "progress," the gods that we believed would provide all the answers, have shown themselves to hold false promises.

Science and technology have extended and increased the power of individuals and groups to an extent undreamed of by our ancestors. The ordinary person in the developed world lives a life of comfort and luxury that most emperors and kings in history could not attain. The rapid access to information and goods, instant communication, and high-speed travel have transformed our lives.

But there is a price to be paid; this power has had an enormous impact on the environment, human rights, and the human condition in general. The major concern we will have to address in the new millennium is not how to increase technological power but how to control it.

Throughout history technological development has always moved itself forward, leaving the moral order trailing behind. In our time technological change and innovation have been so swift and transformative that the moral order has lagged well behind and is now struggling to catch up.

However, the dynamic nature of morality means that it does eventually catch up, and we are now seeing it confront the technological order. People are beginning to rethink moral conventions, to create new values that demand the control and limitation of science and technology.

In this confrontation, ancient Greek philosophy, and in particular Stoicism, is well placed to help us manage our future.

When astronauts brought back photographs of the earth seen from space, the image of our blue and delicate planet floating among the white clouds in its living atmosphere triggered a deep response. Childlike feelings of amazement, wonder, and connectedness that we had lost made this image a spiritual symbol for our age. It stands for the growing awareness that we and the planet are part of a single system; that we can no longer think of ourselves as in some way separate from the natural world.

We now hold the future of the earth in our hands. In the past our efforts were concentrated on harnessing nature, taming nature, keeping nature under control (the very language shows the problem) in order to ensure and promote our survival.

Nature and its great manifestation, Mother Earth, was not brought to her knees when we cut down trees or strip-mined for ore. And now that there are so many of us on the planet, and we have discovered techniques for extracting ore and oil with such ease, and have tampered so badly not only with the forests and the rivers but with the very building blocks of life, we have fooled ourselves into believing we are "the Masters of the Universe." Now that our efforts have gone beyond mere survival into a vast and sophisticated expansion of our concerns, we have the ability to create and destroy life on this planet. But our manipulation of nature threatens to make life intolerable for us.

This raises questions about the relationship between humanity and this beautiful sphere we live on. Are we a kind of global brain and nervous system, whose consciousness can comprehend the consequences of our actions and change them in time to reverse the effects of our worst excesses?

Are all of our activities part of the continuing evolution of this planet? Or are we a planetary cancer, a late malignant growth on the earth, destroying the biological fabric that took so many millennia to create? Will we see the complete destruction of the remaining rain forests? Will we live to see the last of the mountain lions? Will we in fact make this planet uninhabitable?

Whether we become the benevolent consciousness of the earth or its destroyer lies in the will, the desires, and the inner being of every man and woman alive today. The question of survival on earth may well be the ethical question that Socrates asked over 2,300 years ago: "What is the right way to live?"

If we want to survive into the next millennium, we could do worse than take lessons from the Stoics and from Marcus Aurelius on how to live our lives.

MARCUS AURELIUS
(121–180 C.E.)

There have been many great men and women throughout history, but of those who have been involved in affairs of state or business, people whose names have attracted fame and status, Marcus Aurelius is almost unique.

As emperor of Rome from 161 to 180, the sole object of his government, according to the historian Gibbon, was the happiness of its people. No doubt a Roman slave might not have agreed with Gibbon, but even if this happiness applied only to the free men of Rome, it remains an exceptional period in the recorded history of leadership and power.

Plato maintained that the best possible heads of government are philosophers, and Aristotle argued that peoples for whom philosophers legislate are always prosperous. The Roman Empire was lucky enough to find such a man, and wise enough to put him in power.

Abraham Lincoln said that the best way to

test a man's character is to give him power. As emperor of Rome, Marcus Aurelius was the most powerful man in the world. Yet his personal and professional life was dominated by a desire for virtue, justice, and peace, not money, possessions, power, or fame.

MARCUS'S BOOK

The time of Marcus Aurelius's reign may have been a golden age for the Roman Empire, but it certainly wasn't a peaceful one. Besieged on its Asian and German borders by "barbarian" tribes, the empire he ruled was constantly at war.

As commander-in-chief of the Roman armies, he successfully defended these frontiers, subduing local revolts. He returned to Rome in triumph and was made into a kind of saint.

Although he detested war as a disgrace and calamity of human nature, he was forced to spend eight winter campaigns in the field. Camped by the frozen River Danube, he spent his days running the empire from a field tent and witnessing the death and degradation of men at war.

It is remarkable that under these horrendous circumstances Marcus Aurelius was able to spend the dark nights writing a series of thoughts like this:

Gaze in wonder at the ever-circling stars, as if you were floating among them; and consider the alterations of the elements, constantly changing one into another.

Thinking such thoughts you wash away the dust of life on earth.

These thoughts and exhortations were not written for publication or posterity. They were private and personal, a kind of diary for spiritual development.

For the past four hundred years these thoughts of Marcus Aurelius have been called "meditations." They are not really meditations in the sense that we now understand the word. Indeed, the Greek title of the book can be translated as "To Himself." It was probably saved by one of Marcus's friends after his death and circulated among his many admirers.

From the time of his death until the invention of printing, the writings were kept alive by philosophers, Christian theologians, and medieval scholars. *The Meditations of Marcus Aurelius* was first printed in 1558 and has been in constant use ever since, in a great number of languages.

Although we don't know exactly how he wrote, it's very likely that he wrote down his thoughts as and when the need arose, with no overarching plan. Over a period of years, these writings naturally grew into a collection.

This is not a book to be read in a single sitting but one to be dipped into, perhaps at night before going to bed, to find some new thoughts or consolations, or early in the morning before starting the day. Even opening the book at random can lead you to reflect on your existence, the course of your life, the events that are happening to you and how best to handle them.

It's in the nature of books about the spirit that they can be visited again and again. How often we return to books after a gap of some years and find that, with broader experience, we are able to read them in a deeper way, to see new facets that we had previously missed.

Marcus Aurelius's book is one of these—it can't be outgrown; it does not date. It reads in a different way to someone who is twenty than to someone who is sixty yet still has something profound to tell them both about living the *real* good life.

Why has this book retained its power and influence for almost two thousand years, when most classical works have been forgotten? Marcus was writing as a man and not as an emperor. He wrote about his fears and emotions, his sense of the evanescence of life, of despair at the actions of his fellow men and women. In these paragraphs there is nothing about the battles he was fighting with the barbarians or about affairs of state or the great and powerful senators and consuls that he dealt with on a daily basis.

He tried to use his mind to understand what was happening to him every day and to place these events and emotions within the philosophy that he had learned from his teachers. This philosophy is what he relied on to give himself the strength to deal with all events properly, to counsel himself on how to live, how to act, how to prepare for death.

In these attempts to keep balance and harmony in his life, he advises himself on such topics as hope, tolerance, self-sufficiency, harmony, change, perseverance, greed, discipline, confidence, reason, courage, the nature of good and evil, ambition, civility, and man's position in the universe. In this we can see mirrored our own attempts to deal with whatever life throws at us without letting ourselves be overcome by the pain and despair that often accompany life on earth.

Marcus was writing from the heart, and his words vibrate in our souls as we read the thoughts of a man who died over eighteen hundred years ago. His truth remains alive, and the clarity of his mind and being filters down to us almost undiminished by time. We read him as if he were a contemporary figure. Indeed everyone who lives and writes the truth will always remain timely. Fashions may change, and technology may generate new and different societies, but the core of our being stays the same, and the truth of life is always one.

SPIRITUAL EXERCISES

When I was in the midst of writing, I found a book called *Philosophy as a Way of Life* by Professor Pierre Hadot. Hadot has been studying Greek philosophy and Marcus Aurelius for many years, and in his book he emphasizes the point that to the ancient Greeks philosophy was a practice and not an academic study as it is now.

To the ancient Greeks, philosophy (the striving after wisdom) was not a dry, analytical discourse but a means to living life correctly. Philosophy was a tool: a method you could use to maintain harmony in your life, to control negative passions such as anger and hatred, to reason out the best action to take, to understand how the universe worked, and to find your place in it.

Philosophy was to be embraced and lived, not just thought and talked about. The theoretical and discursive parts of philosophy were needed to clarify the mind, but the ultimate purpose was to put these ideas into practice and to live them in the mind, body, and spirit. The philosopher's goal was to live a virtuous life and thereby perfect his or her character and find true satisfaction and happiness. To this end, Marcus Aurelius undertook the writing of his thoughts, to transform his way of living into a purer, more virtuous and contented one. These thoughts were often intended to put daily events and his reactions to them in perspective so that he would know how best to confront similar events in the future. In doing this, he often imagined a view from above, an elevated view of human life, as if looking down from another planet:

In the vastness of the universe, Asia and Europe are just two small corners, all the seas are a single raindrop, and Mount Athos is a little clod; all of present time is but a pinpoint in eternity.

All things are petty, changeable, and perishable. And all things come from beyond, from that universal ruling principle, either directly or as a secondary consequence.

He also exercised his perspective by examining the concept of time. He trained himself to focus his awareness on the present, concentrating on the eternal *now,* turning his attention away from the past and the future to live only in the instant at hand:

Discard everything except these few truths: we can live only in the present moment, in this brief now; all the rest of our life is dead and buried or shrouded in uncertainty. Short is the life we lead, and small our patch of earth.

This perspective gave Marcus a cosmic consciousness, a way of seeing the world as a great unity and as a whole, that widened his response to human affairs.

He also tried to look at things as objectively as possible, avoiding subjective judgments or human sentiments:

Look then at the material objects of life, and consider how trivial and short-lived they are and how often they are owned by scoundrels and thieves. Should you look at the characters of those you live with, it is hardly possible to endure even the best of them, to say nothing of being barely able to stand yourself. In such despair, degradation, and constant confusion of both matter and time, of flux and moving objects, I can hardly imagine finding anything worthy of serious pursuit, much less anything of value.

This gave Marcus the ability to look at things as they really are and not be deceived by conditioned responses or prejudices.

From his writings it is clear that Marcus had a quick temper, and a number of his exercises are about how to deal with anger. He knew that to unleash his anger was wrong since its effect would always harm him more than the person it was directed at. And to bottle it up just increased his frustration. Both of these were harmful to the soul. This was his solution:

> When you are disturbed by events and lose your serenity, quickly return to yourself and don't stay upset longer than the experience lasts; for you'll have more mastery over your inner harmony by continually returning to it.

These writings were intended to exercise Marcus's mind and spirit. Just as the Greeks valued physical exercise as a means to perfect the body, to keep it healthy and develop a strong immune system, so they conceived of spiritual exercise as a way of purifying the soul and perfecting character.

The aim of living one's life was to find contentment, to avoid misery and unhappiness, to find freedom of action and avoid becoming a slave to the "passions," to become self-reliant and independent and not use other people for financial, social, or emotional support.

This is what the ancients believed philosophy was all about. To be a philosopher was to undergo a radical conversion to a lifestyle different from that of other people:

> In the life of man, his time is but an instant, his substance ceaselessly changing, his senses degraded, the flesh of his body subject to decay, his soul turbulent, his fortune difficult to predict, and his fame a question mark. In a word, his body is like a rushing stream, his soul an insubstantial dream, life is warfare, he is a stranger in a foreign land, and even after fame comes oblivion.
>
> How can a man find a sensible way to live? One way and one only—philosophy. And my philosophy means keeping that vital spark within you free from damage and degradation, using it to transcend pain and pleasure, doing everything with a purpose, avoiding lies and hypocrisy, not relying on another person's actions or failings. To accept everything that comes, and everything that is given, as coming from that same spiritual source.

Marcus Aurelius's book of meditations gave him a way of seeing the world and acting within it that provided satisfaction and contentment. Are his ideas and principles only relevant to the Roman world of the second century, or can they be applied to twenty-first-century living? Does Greek philosophy still have something to say to us? Can we improve our lives by listening to it?

HOW THIS BOOK CAME INTO BEING

A couple of years ago, my brothers and I had to move my mother out of the house she had lived in for forty-four years and into a geriatric home. When her things were collected, and mostly thrown out, my high school yearbook turned up. Central High School, Class 216, June 1961. Central had a long history as an academic all-male school in Philadelphia. I hadn't seen the book for years, and I took it home with me and stuck it on the shelf with the family photo albums. A few months later, out of curiosity, I picked it up. I turned to the front of the book, where letters from the principal and our class teacher were printed. This is part of the letter from the principal, Elmer Field:

Many men who have struggled for years to obtain wealth or positions of authority which gave them power over the lives of others have been disappointed and disillusioned. The happiness and satisfaction which they had hoped to gain was not attained. We say that such people were not wise, that they lacked wisdom.

Life is full of problems, and happiness and satisfaction come to us when we are able to judge correctly and make right decisions. Such wise actions are based upon knowledge, and while you have been with us at Central High School, the members of the faculty have tried to make it possible for you to accumulate a store of useful knowledge. In itself this knowledge is not wisdom. It must be applied in all cases with the rights and responsibilities of ourselves and others constantly in mind. There must be a union of head and heart fostered through thoughtful service and companionship with those about us.

As you leave us I hope that the knowledge which you have acquired may be transformed into wise living and that you will grow rapidly in wisdom as the years pass by.

Happiness and satisfaction will then be yours whether you have riches or not.

Our class teacher, the philosophical Joe Phillips, wrote this:

Every age, even ours, has its myths; and where the myths of the ancient Greeks served as lamps to lead them from mere wonder to wisdom, the myths of our time are like walls of mirrors that focus our vision on images of ourselves in selfish and vain solicitation—the myths of happiness and contentment.

We have sought to abolish struggle, frustration, and pain from our lives. We look to our reputation, to our standing among our peers, to our fun and our security. We are ambitious to secure the contradictory components of good health in great luxury, complete freedom with absolute security, and emotional peace from an undisciplined and uncommitted mind.

Born out of folly, this is the myth that will lead us not to the light of wisdom but isolated into the ashes of anguish and regret.

This is the myth that I ask you to forsake without nostalgia, for it demeans the humanity in you. Turn your sights rather to the fact that every new generation is challenged by the press of a different set of circumstances to respond in a timeless way to the problems of men. It has been and is now a call to compassion and sacrifice and love, to a generosity of spirit that is, in a word, the abandonment of self.

The messages they left for us could be straight out of Marcus Aurelius. They reflect their grounding in classical education allied to a Christian upbringing.

But my peers and I had no time for thoughts like these. We were smart, we were clever, we could be cunning, and we knew that the "truth" was that nice guys finish last. Life was a competition in which we were pitted against one another, a dog-eat-dog world where what mattered was money and status. In the world we were going to inhabit, these were the values that would enable us to acquire the things we thought we needed.

On reading their letters, I felt like a Prodigal Son. I had discarded what I had been taught as hopelessly out of date and gone into the world armed with my own ideas about life. Now I had returned and, like the Prodigal Son, I understood that whatever my mistakes and failures, whatever the problems I had caused for myself and others through acting out of ignorance, there was always the possibility of starting afresh, as long as I could recognize the truth and act on it.

Thirty-eight years later, I know that we were wrong and they were right. Their messages may not have been understood at the time, may have been dismissed as old-fashioned, naive, and irrelevant. But their words are still there on the page, and the ideas in those words are still alive, potent, and talking to us today.

We rejected the classical teaching as irrelevant and thought that the new age demanded a new set of answers. No doubt it does, but it may be that the new answers are to be found not by rejecting old and valuable insights but by dusting them off and reexamining them in the light of new experience. In doing so we may be surprised at what we find.

———————

I had first read *The Meditations of Marcus Aurelius* when I was a university student. I found some of the meditations moving and insightful but others difficult to understand. A number of them were obscure and I couldn't fathom the meaning that the author must have intended. The overall impression I had was that this was a thoughtful, deeply serious man who had considered the large questions of existence and had somehow found answers that sustained him.

Two years ago I decided to produce an audiotagpe of Marcus Aurelius's work. I started to read some existing translations but felt that their language was either dated or too steeped in the Christian tradition.

I wanted to have as clear a picture of the original thoughts as possible, but since I do not read ancient Greek I could not even begin to translate the text. I saw a reference to an 1862 translation by George Long, which was said to be completely literal and absolutely correct. This seemed to serve my purpose, and I began to rewrite his antique Victorian English into a contemporary style. At the same time I did not want to lose the sense of Marcus's second-century mind, so I tried to evolve a style that gave meaning to the text in a way that would be useful to a contemporary audience but that still sounded like the words of a Roman emperor. After writing a number of the meditations, I realized that I was producing an entirely new version of Marcus Aurelius.

As I worked on the writing, I could see that Marcus Aurelius had a holistic, cosmic view of life resembling that of the ancient Eastern philosophers. His ability to look objectively at the world and to penetrate deeply into his own mind struck me as similar to the Buddhist approach to psychology. I was also impressed that his perspective on the world was an ecological one, very close to our own view of the link between humanity and the environment.

I realized then that the ideas of the Greek

philosophers have come full circle. The ancient Greeks represent one of the foundations of our culture and civilization. We built on their ideas and in many cases distorted them through our own religious and cultural biases to the point where we rejected the original ideas. But now, just as those letters from my teachers were waiting to be read, we have the chance to return once more to these philosophers, whose truths are undimmed by age. The messages they have for us are not remote intellectual analyses. They saw philosophy as a therapy, as a method for healing souls. As Epicurus said, "Our only occupation should be the cure of ourselves."

Can Greek philosophy provide a remedy for our twenty-first-century malaise?

WHAT IS PHILOSOPHY GOOD FOR?

When we are babies, we have no sense of our own identity, and later we come to share a fluid identity with our mothers. It is only when we become older and more independent that we develop a sense of ourselves, a feeling that we are an "I," a "me," an individual self, with our own thoughts, feelings, and desires. This self is very fragile, built on sand, and as we grow we try to shore it up with as much solidity as we can. We try to make this self happy, and the only way we know how to do this is to follow the ways that our family, friends, teachers, and the media show us. We are formed by what they say and even more so by what they actually do. This cultural conditioning becomes the intellectual environment in which we live. It informs our ideas of how to think and act.

Our main instinct is to survive, to protect this fragile self we have built up. To do this we generally seek pleasure and avoid pain. Seeking pleasure leads us to pursue actions that create emotions of enjoyment and acceptance and make us feel good. Avoiding pain means shunning actions and situations that lead to emotions of suffering: fear, sadness, anger, disgust, and shame. We are led by our desires, and our desires impel us to seek things we do not have and often cannot see. Our objects of desire include other people, money, food, and clothing, as well as more abstract things like fame, love, knowledge, and enlightenment. Our desires are endless and can never be satisfied.

In pursuit of our desires we prefer not to struggle or confront the hard tasks of life. We would like things to be easy, simple, and fun. This often means that we shun problems, sometimes denying that they exist.

But there comes a time in all our lives when, however much we have tried to avoid pain and pursue pleasure, suffering—especially mental anguish—somehow invades our existence.

In the old days religion often provided a cure for this anguish, but in these materialistic and secular times, religion, and the God that is its focus, doesn't seem to provide enough comfort for many people.

Without the solace of God, we are left here on earth with only two kinds of creature comforts to give our lives meaning: intimate loving relationships and satisfying work. These are virtually the only areas of life available in a materialistic culture in which to find satisfaction and contentment.

But satisfying work in our society is very hard to find. Many people must perform soul-destroying work in order to achieve financial security. Many are stressed through insecurity, competition, and anxiety, putting in far too many hours in offices, factories, shops, and on the commute to get there. For many there is no work at all, only the scrap heap of welfare and government programs. And for some people, not even that.

The strain of working too hard and too long and the constant need to make money to pay for ever more things puts stress on our relationships. We don't have enough time for our children, we are too tired to make love, and our energy starts to drain away, leading to a downward cycle of despair, suffering, and illness.

In this state of disharmony and discontent, is it any wonder that people grasp at ever more complex diversions? Music, television, movies, and the Internet keep our minds off life's problems for a while, and if we really need serious escape there is always drink, drugs, or pornography. Most of these distractions cost money, and we have always been taught that money will solve our problems. Many pursue it to the exclusion of everything else, mistaking riches for real wealth. The pursuit of power, fame, and status is another way we continue to bolster our fragile self, trying to create a feeling of permanence, solidity, and security.

We may think that problems like these are a result of modern Western life. But the Romans also lived in a time of spiritual anguish and economic turmoil. They too sought answers to mental suffering and misery through the pursuit of pleasure. The search for happiness and questions of what to value and what to seek are always and everywhere the key human questions.

The Greek philosophers set out to find the answers to these questions and to find a way to rebalance their lives to produce harmony and contentment. Instead of seeing philosophy as an irrelevance to ordinary living, perhaps it is time to apply a therapy from the roots of our own Western tradition to our contemporary spiritual difficulties.

GREEK PHILOSOPHY 101

Marcus Aurelius was a Roman, but his philosophy arose from a Greek tradition that had been practiced for over six hundred years before he began writing. Philosophy in Greece was one aspect of a spontaneous flowering of human spirituality, awareness, and enquiry that appeared simultaneously throughout the civilized world of the fifth century B.C.E. At the same time that philosophers appeared in Greece, the Buddha was seeking enlightenment in India, Confucius and Lao-tzu were discovering The Way in China, and the Prophets of Israel were calling for a renewal of Jewish faith and ethics.

This appearance of Buddhism, Confucianism, Taoism, Greek philosophy, and the renewal of Judaism heralded a new age for humanity, one that opened minds to a fresh conception of the world. There was an understanding that the spirit was not something completely external to humanity, not just a presence out there in the universe, a separate force that inspired feelings of fear and awe, but that this spirit was also internal and inhabited the deepest levels of our being. Through these investigations, various schools of philosophy came into being, of which the most important were Platonism, Aristotelianism, Stoicism, and Epicureanism. Plato set up the first of the schools, the Academy, after the death of his teacher, Socrates. The Academy was a gymnasium where men and boys gathered for physical exercise and philosophical discussions, which flourished in this environment.

Socrates thought that the really important question of life had to do with human conduct and behavior. He wanted to find an answer to the question "What is the right way to live?" He wandered throughout Athens asking everyone he met whether they knew the answer, since he claimed to be ignorant and wanted to secure this knowledge. Socrates became a model for the philosophical life. His followers were united by a desire to live with an attitude to life that, if followed, would allow them to cultivate their inner spirit and provide them with an inner freedom leading to tranquillity and happiness. This could be practiced by anyone, regardless of circumstance.

ZENO–THE FOUNDER OF STOICISM

Socrates separated philosophy into three distinct branches: logic, physics, and ethics.

Logic was used to train the mind to think clearly, to reason and to express thoughts correctly. The main aim was to use logic as a tool with which to discern the true from the false. Without this fundamental discernment all else was useless.

Physics—or nature—was studied to understand how the world operates, to discern the principle of order behind the diversity of nature and see where humanity fits into this scheme. The aim of physics was to inspire the sense of cosmic consciousness that Marcus Aurelius exhibits in his writings, an awareness of nature's laws.

Ethics was the most important branch of study because it involved conduct and behavior and was explicitly involved in answering Socrates' fundamental question, "What is the right way to live?"

Zeno, a semite from Cyprus, probably of Phoenician origin, started as a pupil at the Academy but eventually left and began teaching on his own. Since he could not afford a building, he taught under the shade of a roof or portico, and the name of his school—Stoicism—was derived from the Greek word for roof—*stoa*.

Philosophy—striving after wisdom—was rigorous ethical training. Zeno devised a methodology that combined Socrates' three branches into one system that his students could follow in their everyday activities as a means of perfecting their individual characters. The ideal character was that of a wise man such as Socrates, or the Roman senator Helvidius, who showed remarkable strength of character in dealing with the emperor Vespasian.

Vespasian was once pressuring Helvidius not to attend a sensitive debate in the Senate.

Helvidius said to the Emperor, "It is in your power not to allow me to be a member of the Senate, but so long as I am one, I must go in."

The Emperor replied, "Well, you can go in, but say nothing."

Helvidius: If you do not ask my opinion, I will remain silent.

Emperor: But I must ask your opinion.

Helvidius: And I must say what I think right.

Emperor: But if you do, I shall have you killed.

Helvidius: Have I ever said that I am immortal? You will do your part, and I will do mine: it is your part to kill, it is mine to die—but not in fear; yours to banish me, mine to depart—but without sorrow.

All the Greek schools believed that people are unhappy because they desire things they cannot always attain, and seek after things that are external to their true selves. When people fail to get the pleasurable things they desire, they immediately become miserable, the very thing they had specifically tried to avoid.

Zeno taught his followers that the only thing in life worth pursuing is moral good, or virtue, which is an absolute. The things most people consider good—pleasure, money, fame, status, possessions, power—are neither good nor bad but neutral.

Similarly Zeno held the only evil to be moral evil, another absolute. The only evil in the universe is brought about by the activities of people. But all the things men normally consider bad—poverty, illness, low esteem, death, pain—are also neutral.

Although money, power, and fame do have value in the context of ordinary living, this value was held to be relative to circumstances. Health, wealth, and home are more desirable than illness, poverty, and banishment, but in the interests of true freedom, at times the less desirable option might have to be chosen. The way to happiness and contentment is not to actively pursue pleasure and wealth or to actively avoid pain or poverty but to pursue only the morally good.

Zeno felt that happiness should be sought in freedom of action and of the soul, in desiring only that which is essential to our true selves. As

Socrates had said, "Concern yourself less with what you have than with what you are, so that you can become as excellent as possible."

———◆———

To the Stoic, everything we experience is a matter of judgment. Every evil or fault stems from a false judgment about the world made from ignorance, so that we in effect create our own problems and difficulties. The judgments and decisions we make and the opinions we hold about the world are totally dependent on our state of mind. The ability to judge and decide about events, objects, and people is the only thing we possess that is actually within our power.

The Stoics devised a term for all the things beyond our control: they are *indifferent* to us and should not concern or bother us. For if we try to control something that is not in our power, we will suffer. According to Stoic thought, the things that are not in our power or possession number quite a few:

Our bodies
Our partners and our children
Our friends and colleagues
Our houses, clothes, and all material goods
Our money
Our jobs and worldly power
Our reputation

These are all things that in the course of normal life and conventional thinking we are led to believe are under our control. The Stoics would disagree. Our bodies are not under our control because, although we can move them and dress them, we cannot stop them from becoming ill, aging, and eventually dying. Our partners may leave us; our children may die; our houses may burn down; our material goods may be stolen.

The Stoics believed that although we live with the illusion that these things are under our control, they are really under the control of other people or forces. Whether we become rich or poor, famous or obscure, is dependent on the will and whim of other people and the working out of the circumstances of life.

These circumstances are indifferent to us, but the way we deal with them is not indifferent; it is the essence of our existence.

The key to existence lies in trying to control the things that are actually within our power and subject to our will, which, according to Epictetus, are:

Our judgment and opinions
Our desires
Our adversion, or ability to move toward something
Our aversion, or ability to move away from something

These are all under the control of our will; where we can use our will is where we can find freedom; and the freedom to think and act is the basis of happiness.

Now, when these powers of mind are written out so abstractly they are difficult to understand.

In particular, a word like *adversion* sounds very odd and unfamiliar. But it's possible to look at some of these Stoic ideas through a contemporary lens that is very familiar and that is based on manipulating these same mental powers.

Adversion is the root of a word that we are constantly aware of—*advertising*. The advertising business is as adept as the Stoics in analyzing how our minds work, but it exploits our psychology to sell us things. The images it uses to get us to pay attention are all images of desire, whether sensual or psychological.

In what I would call its positive mode, advertising uses our propensity for desire, and turning toward things, to sell us goods and services. In its negative mode, which uses fear and anxiety, it uses our propensity for aversion, or turning away. For we are averse to—or turn away from—things we don't like, such as shame and pain.

When I am driving down a road, say Sunset Strip in Los Angeles, my eyes can't help but be attracted to the huge billboards advertising the latest movie, CD, car, or airline. And of course, all the things they are trying to sell me belong to the list of things I have no power over: material goods, or status.

Say I have been attracted to a billboard image of a shiny new car on a mountaintop. This sensation registers itself as an image in my brain, and my mind needs to make sense of it, to make a judgment about what is being presented.

The image received is compared with similar images and ideas held in memory. Once the image is identified and classified by comparison with other images, the mind knows what this object is, and I can make a decision about what action to take concerning it. The choices are three: I can go toward this object, turn away from it, or ignore it.

This mental reflex normally happens unconsciously, and we act on the image as quickly as we perceive it. By using the Stoic method, we can train ourselves to slow this process down so that we can actually exercise some control.

So, how would a Stoic go about dealing with this ad? A "representation" has now entered my consciousness, and I need to examine it in an inner dialogue with myself to understand what the image is. I conclude: "It is a photograph of a car on a mountain." A conscious value judgment needs to be made at this point: "Is this thing or idea I perceive under the control of my will or not?" I conclude: "It is an image of a car, a material object, so it is not under the control of my will and is indifferent to me."

Since it is not under the control of my will, I should let the image fade from my brain and not hold on to it. For if I hold on to it and treat it like something under the control of my will, I might think to myself, "My car is a mess. Wouldn't it be great to wheel around in that sleek machine?"

What makes desires so hard to resist are the feelings that images evoke. The company that made the car and the advertisers that created this image want me to feel that this car is a beautiful and powerful object and that I will be powerful and admired if I drive it. Not only that, the striking mountain setting feeds into images of untrammeled nature, which evoke feelings that this car will be a source of freedom and pleasure. I may be driving bumper-to-bumper at 15 miles an hour down a cramped and polluted road, but this new car holds out the promise of speed on clear fresh country roads.

The Stoics would say that the more desires I have, the more things I want, and the more unhappy I will be. If I continually desire things, there is no guarantee that I will acquire them and satisfy this desire. And even if I do acquire them, desire will continue to make new demands. Therefore frustration will set in and with it a host of other ills like anxiety and fear.

Conversely, the fewer my desires, the less I'll want and need, and the happier I will be. If my desires are few, and they are ones that are actually under my control, there is the possibility that I can satisfy them and find true happiness.

The trouble is that our society is based on selling us goods that we don't need, pandering to all our desires, and increasing our wants. Our real needs stay quite small, but by allowing ourselves to be influenced by the commercial demands of society, we increase our false needs and desires and consequently increase our unhappiness.

So my desire for this new car would grow. I would consider how I could pay for it, and if my finances were not up to it, I might have to think about buying it on credit, paying large amounts of interest. To pay the interest I might need to work overtime, or work harder, and see my family less, perhaps, and in any number of ways start to make myself unhappy, either immediately or in the future. And even if I were rich enough to satisfy this desire, other desires would soon come into play: there are always faster and more expensive cars.

Limiting our desires and aversions to those things under our control puts us on the Stoic road to tranquillity and happiness. As Epictetus said,

Remember that if you think things which are by nature dependent (on others) are free, and things which are in the power of others to be your own, you will be obstructed, you will lament, you will be disturbed, you will blame both gods and men; but if you consider only that which is under your control to be your own, and that which is under another's control as belonging to another, as it really is, then no man will obstruct you, you will never blame any man, you will do nothing against your will, you will have no enemy, for you will not suffer any harm.

When you seek what is not your own, you lose what actually is your own.

Most people never make this distinction between what is within their power and what isn't, so they go through life trying to use the world, and the people and objects in it, as a means of satisfying their desires. In contrast to this attitude, the Stoics take a more holistic view of the world, and use their reason and will to secure their happiness.

This emphasis on the mind made Stoicism a lofty and intellectual philosophy. Its appeal to the Greek world was initially to small elite groups of students. After the decline of Athens, the philosophy spread throughout the Greek-speaking cities of Asia Minor. But it was in Roman times that its popularity grew, and it soon became the leading philosophy of the widespread Roman Empire.

MARCUS AURELIUS'S STOICISM

As a teenager Marcus was taught the works of Epictetus, the leading Stoic of the time. Epictetus was a Greek who was brought to Rome as a slave. He was eventually given his freedom by his Roman owner and went on to become an influential philosopher.

Epictetus believed that in all of life's circumstances it was necessary to have ready a set of principles or guidelines that one could apply in order to either take the correct action or else not to act at all and accept one's fate. It is these principles that Marcus is using and writing about in his spiritual exercises. It is his way of keeping them always in mind and applying them to his life:

> When using your principles, emulate the boxer, not the gladiator. For the gladiator must pick up and lay down his sword, but the boxer always has his hands and only needs to clench them.

Epictetus also thought that the philosopher was not to seek wisdom selfishly for his own well-being but put these principles to work in society to enable as many people as possible to benefit. Marcus was aware that as an Emperor he had to maintain his sense of justice as a social duty to his fellow citizens.

The Stoics believed that the lowest and the highest in society, the most humble and the most powerful, the most famous and the most ignominious could think and act in exactly the same way, even under radically differing circumstances. So the power of Stoicism came from a philosophy that could unite a slave and an Emperor.

This was not just theoretical, for the Emperor/philosopher Marcus Aurelius was indirectly the student of the slave/philosopher Epictetus. A philosophy that united these two men must have a great and abiding power.

———— ✦ ————

The Stoics believed that to be able to talk about philosophy meant only that you knew the words.

What you could not demonstrate by talking was how you lived, whether you exhibited these beliefs in your behavior or whether they were only a form of intellectual arrogance.

As Epictetus said,

> Eat like a man, drink like a man, get dressed, get married, have children, lead the life of a citizen. . . . show us all this, so that we can see whether or not you have really learned something from the philosophers.

That this system worked can be seen very clearly in Marcus Aurelius, an able philosopher who applied the Stoic rules to his life and followed the good. Marcus married, had children, looked after his relatives, and did a demanding job, without forgetting the lessons that the Stoics taught him.

Marcus Aurelius did not write anything new about Stoic theory. But since he put Stoic principles into action and *lived* a philosophical life, he has become the best-known example of a Stoic philosopher.

STONE-FACED STOICS

When I told people I was writing on Stoicism, I got reactions like "Oh, that's the stiff upper lip" or "Stoics—they're stone-faced, they don't show their emotions" or "passionless," "a dull, rigid, repressed, musty old-world word."

The usual misconception of Stoicism is that of a gloomy, skeptical, and death-obsessed philosophy that gives its practitioners the ability to endure difficulties and withstand pain and suffering.

Although Stoicism is a philosophy that does give help in difficult times and enables its followers to cope well in times of trouble, this is not its main accomplishment or function.

The Stoic philosophy does consider death and how to face it, but so do all philosophies. Plato even said that philosophy is a training for death. But Stoicism also considers and celebrates life in all its aspects. Fundamentally it says that if you can ally yourself with nature, make yourself at one with nature, it is possible to live a contented life. Death is, of course, part of nature and has to be faced and understood for what it is. But a flower also has to be faced and understood for its qualities.

For the Stoics, life was in fact a festival, something to be enjoyed in full freedom. The teachings of Stoicism were intended to give the person who lived the Stoic life the freedom to enjoy life at every moment in the fullest possible way.

Epictetus thought that good people would say to God when they were dying,

> I leave full of gratefulness to you, for you have judged me worthy of celebrating the festival with you, of contemplating your works, and of following together with you the way in which you govern the world.

Gloom and doom are not the essence of this philosophy. Living a philosophical life may have made the Stoic a more serious and attentive person, but the Stoics believed that to live any other way—not to live a philosophical life—was to live in misery, at war with oneself.

The misconceptions about Stoicism miss the fact that it offers a vital, radical, and fresh view of the world and a vibrant, empowering way of living in it—one that shows us that the key to peace and tranquillity is completely in our own hands.

HOW THIS BOOK IS PRESENTED

Marcus Aurelius's meditations are traditionally divided into twelve chapters, the first being autobiographical in nature and the remaining eleven containing a variety of his thoughts, in no particular order. I have made a selection of about half of his original spiritual meditations and have given each individual text a title so that it will be easier for readers to locate a particular thought for reference.

The individual texts I have grouped into eight chapters, according to the ideas they express:

Chapter 1   Living in the World
Chapter 2   Cultivating the Self

Chapter 1: Living in the World

Carved on the Temple of the Oracle at Delphi in ancient Greece were the words "Know yourself." Socrates, the greatest of the Greek philosophers, following this precept, said, "The unexamined life is not worth living."

To examine your life and to seek to know yourself is to find out the inner truth about your "self" and your existence. It is a matter of making an inner journey, of taking the deepest inner view until you reach even the unconscious levels of the mind. It is a question of going down and looking below the level of the ego, of the "I." If you can make this journey and find this truth, the question "What is the right way to live?" can be answered.

When Socrates asked, "What is the right way to live?" he was asking a practical question as well as an ethical question since the problem of the right way to live is a question of ethics. Aristotle said we study ethics not because we want to know what goodness is but so that we can *become* good. Marcus expressed this view:

> If you can work sincerely and correctly on what is at hand, and do so with energy and calm, not allowing distractions but keeping your inner spirit pure, as if you had only borrowed it and had to return it intact; if you can act in this way, hoping for nothing, fearing nothing, but satisfied with modulating your actions to the way of nature, and with fearless truth in every word you utter, you will live contentedly.

Marcus's teacher Epictetus said that the ultimate aim of the practice of Stoicism was to become like the wise man or sage. It was thought that no one could actually become a sage, but by trying to emulate the impossibly good and virtuous figure of the wise man and living your life in a philosophical way, you could make a great deal of progress in the development of your character.

This is what we see Marcus Aurelius trying to do in this chapter. He had to deal with the pressures and problems of war and empire, and we find him using his Stoic principles to cope with them. He sought to learn how best to act justly to other people and how to relate to work and society while living in the world.

Chapter 2: Cultivating the Self

What are these Stoic principles that Marcus Aurelius was using? Stoicism had existed for over four hundred years, and the Stoics had worked out their idea of how human nature works. They had established methods to guide conduct so that people could constantly refine their characters and lead a life of tranquillity and contentment.

At the heart of Stoic philosophy lies rationality:

> . . . not to yield to the impulses of the body, for it is the property of reason and the intellect to

limit itself and not be overpowered either by the senses or impulses, which are the animal in us. The mind claims superiority and does not permit itself to be overpowered by the others; and with good reason, for it is formed by nature to use all of them.

The Stoics saw humanity at its highest level as being completely ruled by reason, which meant overcoming the unfortunate tendency to overrule and override reason with the "passions."

For us the word *passions* implies strong emotions or feelings, which we usually see as positive and vibrant states of mind and body. But the Stoics defined passions as excessive impulses or desires that could overcome rationality and create a "disturbance of the soul." Once the soul is disturbed and in turmoil, imbalance occurs and equilibrium is lost.

The Stoics regarded the passions as similar to physical illness; they cause a kind of fever and then pass on. Like illness, they can and should be prevented. Just as medicine treats illnesses of the body, so philosophy can treat illnesses of the soul. The philosopher was seen as a "doctor of the soul."

The Stoics believed that every desire that is not morally good can be dangerous if taken to excess. For example, the idea that money is good can easily lead to an excessive pleasure in the obtaining of money—greed. And to live continuously driven by this passion of greed eventually leads to avarice. Such passions are distortions of our natural state of humanity and obstacles to good character. Marcus Aurelius commands himself:

> Concentrate on your mind, your ruler. You are old; it's time to stop your mind acting like a slave, pulled puppetlike by the strings of selfish desires.

To pursue only the morally good was seen to be sufficient for satisfaction, contentment, and happiness in living. To Marcus Aurelius the saying "virtue is its own reward" means that the feeling of pleasure in being virtuous is a real pleasure—a kind of bliss or joy:

For what can be more pleasant than wisdom itself, when you consider the safety and contentment of everything that relies on our mind's understanding and knowledge?

Clearly, philosophers like Marcus Aurelius had a view of the world that is radically different from ours. They wanted to live a rational and objective life and to lose the irrational and subjective perception that most people have of the world. They tried to replace the uncertainty of fleeting pleasure with a more enduring feeling of joy in pure existence.

Their methods aimed at infusing the mind with serenity and tranquillity to replace the chaos, frustration, and anguish that represents existence for many people. Marcus Aurelius saw philosophy as the only thing that could cure this mental and spiritual suffering.

Chapter 3: The Inner Spirit

Marcus Aurelius instructed himself to:

> Dig inside; inside is the fountain of good, and it will forever flow, if you will forever dig.

Dig inside; look closely; know yourself.

Rodger Kamenetz, in his book *The Jew in the Lotus,* tells the story of a group of people who visited the late Hasidic rabbi Menachem Mendel Schneersohn in Brooklyn.

> One of them asked the Rabbi starkly, "What are you good for?" And the Rabbi said, "I'm not talking about myself, I'm talking about what my Master was for me. He was for me the geologist of the soul. There are great treasures in the soul: there's faith, there's love, there's awe, there's wisdom, all these treasures you can dig, but if you don't know where to dig, you dig up mud.
>
> "But if you want to get to the gold, which is the awe before God, and the silver, which is the love, and the diamonds, which are the faith,

then you have to find the geologist of the soul who tells you where to dig . . . . But the digging you have to do yourself."

People today, brought up in a skeptical, secular, and scientific world, are going to ask of their soul and spirit, "What are you good for?" When everything else has to pay its way, when what is seen as worthless is so easily discarded, the soul and spirit must convince people that they are worth holding on to, that they have a value.

How can we find this value? Where are our geologists of the soul? Epictetus said,

Zeus has placed by every man a guardian, every man's inner spirit, to whom he has committed the care of the man, a guardian who never sleeps, is never deceived. For to what better and more careful guardian could he have entrusted each of us?

Marcus Aurelius put it like this:

Those who live with the gods always show their souls to be satisfied with the life assigned to them. They constantly follow the dictates of their spirit, the same spirit that Zeus has given to each one of us as a guardian and guide.

And this spirit is our mind and reason.

When Crosby, Stills, Nash, and Young sang with Joni Mitchell, "We are stardust, we are golden" at Woodstock in 1969, I thought it was just a songwriter's poetic idea. Later, when I read about the origins of our planet, I realized that there could be a deeper meaning.

The earth, and everything on it, had really been created from stardust, flung out from some huge stellar explosion. The earth had started life as a fiery ball of burning debris—stardust—and *Homo sapiens,* wise man, was the end result of a long chain of adaptation and evolution.

The stardust that we are made of links us with everything else on earth created from stardust: the rocks, plants, and animals that we share our planet with and live among.

Given that we are made of the same basic elements that make up water, trees, or rocks, where did consciousness come from? What miracle of growth and creation has managed to create the ability to think and to be self-aware? How can we account for our feelings and emotional sensitivity? Where did they come from?

Our inner spirit is the link between the microcosm of humanity and the macrocosm of the vast universe. The ancient Greeks thought that the inner spirit of humanity was an emanation of the great universal spirit. Because mankind shares this spirit with the gods, we are able to perfect our morality and seek wisdom.

It was by keeping his spirit free from error that Marcus Aurelius could find freedom and serenity:

> . . . nothing will happen to me that is not in harmony with the nature of the universe; and it is in my own power never to act against my God and inner spirit . . .

Chapter 4: The Universal Mind

For our ancient ancestors, nature was unpredictable and dangerous. Even with all our modern technology, floods and drought can still wipe out crops and cause famine, strong winds blow down trees and demolish homes, and earthquakes, hurricanes, and tornados destroy whole villages and towns. But because of scientific knowledge, we are content to call this nature at work and do not believe in malevolent spirits.

To ancient people, these natural phenomena seemed supernatural. They were forces that had a will of their own. The sun, sky, earth, wind, and water were all gods that man had to appease in some way. Everything that man could not identify with himself was thought to contain a spirit of some kind.

Religion developed to give humanity a way to deal with these wayward spirits. Sacrifices, at first of humans, later of animals, and then of fruits were made and prayers recited to ensure prosperous harvests and avert disasters.

The first ancient Greek religion was the worship of trees, stones, and animals, which all contained gods representing natural forces. When an ancient Greek looked at a grove of trees and imagined a spirit inhabiting it, he was making sense of the power of nature. He was in fact projecting onto the trees his own sense of energy and life. Mankind at this time was not self-aware, did not see it was human consciousness being placed in the tree and then reflected back and sensed as the power of that tree.

Because the Greeks thought that humanity and the human form were everything, their gods eventually developed a human shape and human characteristics. In the second stage of Greek religion, the sun, sky, earth, and all the other forces were given names and characters, and a mythology developed to make sense of the wayward action of nature. These gods, like Zeus, Athena, and Poseidon, were thought to live in the heavens on Mount Olympus.

In practice this religion was completely ritualistic. One had only to pray, make offerings, and give sacrifices to the gods to fulfill their demands. There was no spiritual doctrine, and no moral precepts emanated from the gods.

Later, when the Greek mind became more sophisticated and self-aware, the thinkers of the day became dissatisfied with the traditional mythology. They saw that in action the gods were liars, fornicators, and deceivers and neither provided nor inspired spiritual beliefs.

The Olympian gods had also become so numerous and confusing that no one could keep track or make sense of them. The idea then developed that just as Greek civilization was a fusion of many races and ideas, so the gods were really parts of a single divine force, a unity that was mysterious and undefinable. This divine force or divinity operated through nature and controlled fortune and destiny.

Because their gods had no spiritual message, the philosophers could no longer give them credence and looked elsewhere for an expression of their deepest beliefs. Interest in philosophy and science evolved.

After all their searching and questioning, philosophers like Socrates and the Stoics saw "mind" or "reason" as the principle behind everything and immanent in everything. Reason was the directing and organizing force in the universe. It had originated the universe from a single seed and arranged everything that we could see: the movements of the stars, the growth of a flower, the beating of our hearts. Everything was caused by mind operating through nature and destiny.

God was reason. Not a personal anthropomorphic god like Zeus and not a god standing outside creation like the Jewish God, this god of reason was like the ultimate sage. Since universal reason pervades all of creation with thought, the Stoics and other groups of philosophers assumed there must be a thinker, a sagacious mind that had created the world and that predetermined all things.

Reason as a universal principle is found in nature and in all of her creations. It is found in our individual natures and thus in the organization of our societies. Reason as an ordering principle has certain beginnings and endings; it represents an organic pattern of causes and conditions that runs through everything in existence. The Stoics saw human reason as an emanation of universal reason, just as our inner spirit was an emanation of the universal spirit. Nature was no less than all of reality, which flowed from her according to the fundamental principle of reason.

Today many of us have difficulty with the term *reason* because it implies an attempt to control nature—both human and universal—through the use of rational thinking only. It means the use of a linear logic that has led to a world many of us believe is seriously flawed.

Such an arid approach has caused an imbalance in our way of living, which has led to disharmony in our society as well as in our bodies and souls. This disharmony is seen dramatically in slavery, concentration camps, and wars, and also in everyday life in things like industrial pollution and a widespread spiritual malaise.

When Marcus Aurelius used the word *reason* or *rational,* he had in mind an ecological view of creation and the universe. He saw the world as a place where there was an interconnection and interdependency of all things with each other; where the cooperation and integration between human, animal, and vegetable worlds originated in the principle of reason that ran through the entire cosmos.

The Stoics believed that because we have consciousness and can therefore think in the same way that the universe thinks, human beings hold a privileged position. We are able to reflect on creation like the gods, and we can use our minds and bodies to create in the same way that nature creates.

We all share in this universal reason, and we share its order and rationality. Individually, it is seen as the soul or inner spirit or intelligence or mind. It is not a reduced and limited form of what we call thinking, but a holistic view of all creation, a cosmic view of nature and the creative force of reason.

Chapter 5: Contemplating Death

When I was ten, my father died of a heart attack. He was nearly fifty. His death was for many years the most influential and important event in my life, causing a complete transformation of almost everything I knew: the car was sold, we moved to a new neighborhood, money was tight, holidays sparse, and Mom went out to work.

A few years ago, I had my fiftieth birthday party—a happy event. After the last stragglers had gone and the mess was cleared, my wife and I sat at the kitchen table, talking. Inevitably, I remembered my father, who never had a chance to celebrate his fiftieth birthday surrounded by love. How much he missed. How much he was missed.

I realized that the innocent and naive ten-year-old boy who had been, and still, in some way, was me, had thought that since my father died at forty-nine, I was bound to follow suit. This idea had stayed buried in me for forty years, and although I had glimpsed it peeking out at odd moments during all that time, it was only now that I recognized it had been real but was now past its sell-by date.

Parties are important rituals, and this one brought the reality of being fifty right in my face. I had actually made it to fifty, and I was still breathing! Not only that, but at forty-nine, instead of dying, I had become a father again and had a wonderful baby daughter. So life, instead of contracting to its expected end, was expanding and being renewed. My time had yet to come.

This realization started me thinking about the meaning of death. Many people fear death because they fear the unknown. The idea of the void, of nothingness, terrifies them. Others don't want to leave the pleasures of the world behind.

Death takes us away from everything we love. It is the ultimate separation. We fear being alone forever. Can we say, as the Stoics would, "I thank life, whatever it brings me; I thank this great nature for everything I have"? In this attitude we find serenity, tranquillity, and contentment. Life has nothing more to offer us than what it already has. Its bounty is endless.

As Thich Nhat Hahn, the great Zen Buddhist says, "The miracle is not to walk on water, the miracle is that we can walk on earth." Wouldn't it be fine to have that sense of the miraculous in everyday life, to wake up just happy to be alive, satisfied with breathing. Can we find the simple satisfaction of the Buddhist monk who said, "Every day is a good day"?

We treat death as a tragedy, as an ending of the good times. But what if we could think of it as it really is in nature, a process of physical change, an inevitable transformation, something you cannot alter and so must accept. Then it's possible to look directly at it instead of turning away in fear, to examine it instead of shunning it in denial. This is how Marcus Aurelius viewed it:

> Do not fear death, but welcome it, since it too comes from nature. For just as we are young and grow old, and flourish and reach maturity, have teeth and a beard and gray hairs, conceive, become pregnant, and bring forth new life, and all the other natural processes that follow the seasons of our existence, so also do we have death.

A thoughtful man will never take death lightly, impatiently, or scornfully, but will wait for it as one of life's natural processes.

This attitude of Marcus Aurelius was shared by philosophers everywhere and is beautifully illustrated by this Taoist story:

When his great friend Hui-Tzu heard that the sage Chuang Tzu's wife had died, he immediately went to console him. But when he arrived at Chuang Tzu's house he found him singing and drumming on an old tub in front of his wife's coffin.

Hui-Tzu was shocked, and said, "When a wife has lived with her husband and raised children, and then dies in old age, it would be difficult to hold back tears. But isn't it a bit extreme to sing and drum?"

Chuang Tzu said, "No, it's not. When she first died, it was impossible for me not to mourn for her like everyone else. But then I reflected on the very beginning of her existence when she had not yet been born. Not only had she no life, but she had no bodily form; not only had she no bodily form, but she had no breath.

"Because of the intermingling of yin and yang, there ensued a change, and she had breath; another change, and there was her bodily form; another change, and there came birth and life. Now there is another change, and she is dead. The relation between these things is like the procession of the four seasons from spring to summer, from autumn to winter.

"Now she lies at peace in her coffin, and if I were to fall about sobbing and wailing, it would look as if I did not understand the ways of destiny. I therefore controlled myself."

Plato said that philosophy was an exercise and training for the ultimate human experience: death. His teacher, Socrates, had shown the greatest bravery and courage in the face of his own death, and he said at the time that "those who go about philosophizing correctly are in training for death, and they, above all men, are the least frightened of it."

To come to an acceptance of death, the inevitable ending of his time, gave Marcus Aurelius the possibility of facing death calmly and with serenity, and of living a life free from fear of it.

Chapter 6: Everything Changes

When the ancient Greek philosophers looked at the world and saw its diversity and the seeming chaos of things, they looked for what was primary, the first principle, what gave unity or order to all these differences. They looked for a universal substance that could be the basis of everything.

Thales thought this primary substance was water and that everything originated from it. Anaximenes who followed him said it was air, and later Heraclitus said it was fire.

The Stoics took the view that Heraclitus was correct and that fire was the basic element since fire is always found in movement or flux or change, which is universal.

Heraclitus thought that the world is composed of fire in its many transformations of shape and form. His belief was that everything is always moving, is always changing, and thus is in a constant state of *becoming* rather than a state of static being. We are all in transition, never static or at rest but always in a state of process or transformation.

The idea of water or air or fire being the substance from which everything else is derived sounds to us like a very naive form of science. But if you reflect further, you realize that our world started as a great ball of fire before it cooled, that the sun, our source of life, is in essence fire, and if the universe did start its existence with a big bang, then fire does not seem so far off from some kind of first principle.

In fact, as Werner Heisenberg, the nuclear physicist, said, "Modern physics is in some way extremely near to the doctrines of Heraclitus. If we replace the word *fire* with the word *energy*, we can almost repeat his statements word for word from a modern point of view." Modern science catches up with ancient wisdom.

Energy is the universal potency found in all elementary particles and therefore is the basis from which all things are made, and energy manifests as constant movement. So although Heraclitus and the Stoics were wrong in their assumption that fire was the universal substance, their interpretation of fire, that it constantly changed and transformed, was correct, and their view of the nature of the world tallies with our contemporary knowledge.

Heraclitus also said, "You can't step into the same river twice," since the water you stepped into the first time will have flowed away by the time you step in again. The entire universe is never the same from one instant to the next. We too are subject to the constant process of change, never staying the same from moment to moment, however hard we may fight to arrest this change.

Change was a constant theme for Marcus Aurelius:

> Why should anyone be afraid of change? What can take place without it? What can be more pleasing or more suitable to universal nature?
>
> Can you take your bath without the firewood undergoing a change? Can you eat without the food undergoing a change? And can anything useful be done without change?
>
> Don't you see that for you to change is just the same, and is equally necessary for universal nature?

And this is what he thought of its processes:

> All particles of matter soon disintegrate into the substance of the whole; and every form or cause integrates into the primordial; and the memory of all things is swiftly overwhelmed in eternity.

Although Marcus Aurelius was not concerned with the scientific side of philosophy, the fact that Stoic science was basically correct underpins the validity of his ideas. This is one of the reasons why his words are still relevant to contemporary life.

Chapter 7: At One with Nature

Epictetus said,

> You are a human being, and a human being is a mortal animal that has the power of using appearances [or the phenomena of life] rationally. And what I mean by *rationally* is completely conformably to nature. The unique thing

that you possess is the rational faculty. Adorn it and beautify it.

To Marcus Aurelius what is natural is conformity with the order and reason of universal Nature:

> Our universal Nature is the Nature that pervades all existence, and everything that now exists has a kinship to all other things that will come into existence. This universal Nature is called truth and is the original creator of all truths.

By using reason we can act according to nature and live a life of seamless harmony. But reason can be both good and bad. There is right reason and wrong reason. How can we know which is right reason? And besides, what exactly is *nature*?

Our idea of nature is the tamed countryside. But for city dwellers, grass doesn't grow underfoot, animals are pets or are found in the zoo, and water comes out of taps. It is dark when we turn the lights out, not when the sun disappears. Our food comes from supermarkets, wrapped in packaging.

We feel cut off from nature, alienated from it. Our lives are lived in a more artificial, synthetic way. We may desire organic food and cotton shirts, but our lives are still man-made. The natural rhythms of life seem far removed from us. How can we feel what those rhythms are?

After Heraclitus said that the world was made of fire and its transformations, two later Greek philosophers, Leucippus and Democritus, said that the world was made out of atoms, the indivisible smallest units of matter.

This idea of atoms as the fundamental building blocks of matter survived for over two thousand years. Isaac Newton saw these material particles as small solid and indestructible objects. They were passive and had no soul or mind, but the entire world was constructed of them.

Then, two hundred and fifty years later, the first experimental evidence for the existence of basic particles emerged, and they were hailed as the "atoms" of Democritus.

In Fritjof Capra's book *The Tao of Physics,* he describes what happened when the atomic physicists at the turn of the last century had the technical capability to penetrate the atom. They were astounded by what they found. It turned out that atoms were not hard and solid but in fact contained vast areas of space in which extremely minute particles called electrons moved around a nucleus at tremendous speed.

There was a strange and unexpected reality to the atom. As scientists looked closer at the electrons, it seemed that these too were nothing like the solid objects of classical physics. Depending on how they are observed, they appeared sometimes as particles and sometimes as waves.

This uncertainty at the heart of matter and the chance nature of these atomic occurrences were completely unexpected and led to the realization that matter is a complicated set of relations between all the parts of the universe. This means that there is a basic oneness to the universe, with everything partaking of this dual particle/wave aspect of matter.

Inside the atom is mass/energy, constantly in motion, in effect the same energy that Heraclitus had postulated. This energy is the link between our individual selves and the universe. We are self-coherent, self-organizing living systems linked by the energy in our atoms. Marcus Aurelius could sense this:

> Constantly regard the universe as a single living being, having one substance and one soul; observe how all creation relates to the cosmic consciousness of this one living being.
>
> Observe too how everything moves with its impulse, working together to create all events, continuously spinning its delicate thread in the amazing complexity of its web.

Atoms act the same whether they make up our bodies, a table, or a stone. All of nature is made up of these atoms, so there is no need for us to strive to follow Nature, since our nature is the same nature that runs through the universe. It acts no differently in us than it does in any other creature or object.

We are at one with Nature since we *are* Nature. The same energy that makes our heart beat shines the sun. Whatever makes our nervous system work also makes lightning; the wind and our breath are the same; our eyes exist because light waves shine down from the sky.

To be in accord with Nature means to observe how it works—its patterns of growth and development, the process of transformation as things alter from state to state—and to act accordingly. To understand that we do not live outside of Nature is to tap into a wellspring of harmony and contentment.

Chapter 8: Peace Is in Your Hands

Until the time of Neoplatonism, Stoicism was the most highly spiritual form of philosophy in ancient Greece and Rome. It was so spiritual that it is as accurate to call it a religion as a philosophy.

Marcus Aurelius writes about God, sometimes referring to Zeus and at other times to the originator and creator of the universe. When he mentions the gods, he is usually referring to the Olympian gods. Epictetus's most famous saying is "What can I do, a lame old man, save sing God's praise and call on all men to join me in my song." God was never far from their minds.

Nietzsche says that what "is so astonishing in the religious life of the Greeks is the irrestrainable stream of *gratitude* that it pours forth." The Greeks were immensely pleased, grateful, and astonished that God had created a world in which there was, as Hadot says, such "a miraculous coincidence between the needs of living beings and the facilities provided for them by nature."

To the Stoics the fact that there existed colors and light, objects that reflected them, and eyes to see them, with all of them working together, showed the work of a creator and not just nature. It was Reason, the rational principle and the intelligence of God that created order in the universe.

To the Stoics anything that existed implied a maker, and even if that maker was unseen, its presence was undeniable in the face of its works. The amazement and wonder they felt at the sight of these works of nature all fitting so well together for man's benefit gave them a tremendous sense of gratitude and contentment.

However, it is not necessary to have a belief in God or to believe in the spiritual values of the Stoics to use their system of philosophy. This system is a practical method of discovering how to live and needs no supernatural basis of beliefs to be effective.

For Marcus Aurelius the universe was one perfect harmony, above all things to be loved. It was God's abode, was in fact God. Marcus had an enthusiastic acceptance of Nature and the universal law. His attitude to God was one of worship and love.

Philosophy became, in a way, the third religion of Greece. It was a religion without ritual or priesthood, though Marcus Aurelius realized that each individual philosopher made himself holy through the activities of his mind:

For such a man, who tries to live by the right values, becomes a priest and servant to the gods, using the spirit that is embedded within him, which makes him unsullied by pleasure, impervious to pain, untouched by insults, feeling no wrong; a warrior in the best fight, one who cannot be overcome by any desires, with a deep love of justice, and accepting with all his soul everything that happens to him as his great destiny.

By using reason and judgment to gain control over his mind and body, Marcus Aurelius was able to sustain an inner harmony and serenity that carried him joyfully through life.

In an age when we are conditioned to have everything and to want even more, to seek no limitation on the desires of the mind and the body, this has become a revolutionary idea.

In this century that is just beginning, we may find that it is in the control of our desires that we can find the inner freedom for a different kind of happiness than the one we have been seeking. This happiness may give us the internal peace that we yearn for yet find so difficult to achieve.

PHILOSOPHY MAKES A COMEBACK

In our search for answers to the perpetual questions of human existence, we have looked in countless places. There is hardly a region of the globe or a cultural group that has not been ransacked in our search for relief of our eternal anguish.

In recent years we've been looking to the ancient Eastern philosophies of India, China, Japan, and Tibet to quench our thirst for understanding. The list of available therapies, prescriptions, and practices grows daily in what has become a supermarket of the soul.

Traditional religions no longer seem to provide an answer, since they are no longer talking to the inner person. They are now seen as things of the world, self-perpetuating institutions unable to address the contemporary soul. There is a need for revitalization of the spirit in the face of a heartless materialism.

We are now searching for meaning without dogma, for a bedrock of wisdom without laws and regulations. Stoicism seems to answer this need perfectly. It provides a method and a practice that is not dependent on ritual or traditions but relies solely on a love of wisdom and practical methods to achieve it. It offers a tried and tested way to gain control over our lives and gives help in our quest for satisfaction and happiness.

Now, perhaps, in coming full circle, the attention of our society is returning to the origins of Western civilization. Philosophy has found a new audience and has been described as "the intellectual equivalent of Ralph Lauren combat trousers."

In our time the most powerful forces in society are no longer presidents, prime ministers, and monarchs, but immense multinational corporations. Even these all-powerful organizations sometimes feel the need for sage advice and have called in philosophers to lecture their executives and staff.

One such philosopher is Tom Morris, who recently wrote a book called *If Aristotle Ran General Motors*. In his book, Morris quotes the controversial statement that General Motors president Charles Erwin Wilson made in 1952:

"What's good for the country is good for General Motors, and what's good for General Motors is good for the country."

Although Morris says that this statement was received at the time as "perverse" and "a shameless expression of corporate hubris," he goes on to say that "there are some basic truths, discernible by philosophical reflection, which undergird any sort of human excellence or flourishing," and these truths will show that, at bottom, "what's good for the country is indeed good for General Motors, and that what's good for General Motors is very good for the rest of us as well."

I don't agree with Tom Morris's conclusions, and in this new century we would have to substitute some other company to make sense of Wilson's 1952 statement and Morris's judgment about it. For example, what's good for the country may indeed be very good for Microsoft or Monsanto, but is the reverse also true—that what's good for Microsoft or Monsanto is good for the country? Surely the interests of large multinationals and the interests of ordinary people cannot always be the same?

In Britain, the new government, hand in hand with Monsanto and other companies, tried to introduce genetically modified foods into the country after a very short period of tests and trials. Individual consumers objected and told the supermarkets that they would refuse to buy genetically modified foods if they were on offer. The supermarkets, faced with defiant consumers, quickly announced that they had decided not to use genetically modified foods in their own brands and told the government to think again about the speed with which these new and untested foods were being introduced. The government backed down.

Ordinary people believed that what was good for Monsanto was definitely not good for the country, and they made their wishes known. Individual consumers had an image of the food that they would be eating, reflected that the decision about what they would eat was under their own control (or if not completely under their control, at least more under theirs than under Monsanto's), and came to a judgment: we don't trust this food and we don't want it.

This is real philosophy in action, and it is small, seemingly insignificant acts like this—individuals making judgments about what they will eat, what they will buy, how they will travel, and what they will make at work—that can determine the future of our planet.

By acting on these judgments, and by examining and questioning the control that other people, such as governments, institutions, authorities, and the ubiquitous and all-powerful multinationals, have over our lives, we will be able to decide whether humanity is a positive consciousness or a negative cancer on the world.

Philosophy, as a way of reclaiming our minds, is perhaps the first and most important step on the road to regaining some form of control over our lives.

Because we really are "the Masters of the Universe," and the future of the planet lies in our hands.

London
April–September 1999

PART TWO

❋

THE SPIRITUAL TEACHINGS OF MARCUS AURELIUS

❋

❖ 1 ❖

LIVING
IN THE
WORLD

❖

AGAINST NATURE

Begin each day by saying to yourself, "Today I shall meet people who are interfering, ungrateful, arrogant, deceitful, envious, and selfish." They are made this way because of their ignorance of what is good and evil.

But I, who have seen the nature of good and its beauty, and of evil and its ugliness, know that the inner nature of the man who does evil is the same nature as mine (not that we are brothers, but we possess the same mind and the same share of spirit); therefore I can't be harmed by any of these men, for no one can impose on me what is degrading.

I shouldn't be angry with my brother or hate him. For we are made to work in harmony, like a man's two feet or hands, eyelids, or the rows of upper and lower teeth. To work against one another is against Nature; and it is acting against Nature to be angry and to turn away.

TAKING AIM

Are you distracted by the things of the world?

Give yourself some quiet time to discover something new, and learn how to stop this restlessness.

And beware that you don't fall into another kind of error: the folly of those who wear out their lives in ceaseless business, but have no aim on which their every action or thought is focused.

THE TRUE AIM

Always try to persuade people; but if the principles of justice show the way, you must act even against their will.

If, however, someone employs force to resist, then take a different approach: maintain your contentment and tranquillity, and use this obstacle as a chance to exercise another virtue; remember that your attempt was always with a reservation, and you were not aiming for the impossible.

What was your aim? To act in a moral way. Then you succeeded, even if what you wanted to accomplish did not come to pass.

———•———

WORK AND REST

Work hard, but not like one who is distressed, or as someone wanting pity or admiration. Desire only one thing—to act or to rest, as your reason requires.

———•———

THE REAL VALUE OF WORK

When you have to drag yourself out of bed in the morning, keep this in mind: I'm getting up to do the work of a human being. Why be dissatisfied if

I'm going to do the things that I was brought into this world to do? Or have I been made to loll back in the warm sheets?

"It is more pleasant."

Is your existence only for pleasure and not for activity or work? Don't you see the little flowers, the birds, ants, spiders, and bees working together to put in order their own bit of the Universe? Are you unwilling to do the work of a human being and not rush to do what your nature commands?

"But it's also necessary to take rest."

Yes, it's necessary, but Nature has fixed limits to this too. She has fixed limits both to eating and drinking, and yet you go well beyond these limits, past what is needed. But with your actions this isn't so, since your efforts fall far short of your abilities. So clearly you don't love yourself, for if you did you would love your nature and its will.

Those who love their own talents exhaust themselves in working at their skill, unwashed and without food, but you value your own nature less than the carpenter values his woodwork, or the dancer her dance or the greedy man money, or the boastful man a bit of fame. And such people, when they have a strong affection for something, choose not to eat or sleep but rather to perfect the things they care for.

———— ◆ ————

DOING MY DUTY

I do my duty. Nothing else can distract me; for it will either be something lifeless or irrational, or someone who has gone astray and wandered off the true path.

———— ◆ ————

SEEING WEALTH FOR WHAT IT IS

Accept prosperity without pride, and always be ready to let it go.

MEETING CHALLENGES

Just because you find something difficult to do, don't think that it's humanly impossible. If something is humanly possible and appropriate, believe that it can also be attained by you.

GENTLE COMBAT

Suppose that during a game someone has scratched you, or has banged your head and inflicted a wound. Well, you would try not to show any signs of anger, or become offended, or suspect your opponent afterward of being spiteful. Yet you would become wary of him, not as an enemy, or with suspicion, and gently avoid that player.

Your behavior in all spheres of life should be like this; let's overlook many things in those who are, in a way, our fellow contestants. For it's in our power to avoid them, and to have no suspicion or ill will.

———•———

THE RIGHT THING

When you are upset by a man's despicable conduct, immediately ask yourself, "Is it possible for despicable people not to exist?"

"No, it's not possible."

Then don't expect the impossible. For this person is just one of many depraved people who must exist in the world.

Think the same way about the villain, the

cynic, and every fool you meet. For when you remind yourself that unfortunately such people do exist, you will become more kindly disposed toward them.

Reflect also on what qualities nature has given us to counter every vile act. For she has given us compassion as an antidote to brutality, and for another affliction some other quality. And in each case it's possible for you to correct the person who's gone astray; for everyone who errs misses the mark and goes down the wrong path.

Besides, how have you suffered? You'll find that none of these people have done anything to harm your mind, for everything that is harmful and evil to you has its existence only in the mind. Why do you find it strange that an uncultivated person acts like an idiot?

Perhaps you should blame yourself since you didn't expect this man to err in such a way. Your inner voice should have told you it was likely that he would commit this error, and yet you didn't pay attention and are now amazed that he has erred.

But most of all, when you blame someone

for being faithless or ungrateful, turn to yourself. The fault is clearly your own, if you trusted that he would keep his promise, or offered your own kindness only because you expected to gain by it.

For what more do you want when you have done someone a service? Shouldn't you be content that you have done the right thing, and not feel you have to be paid for it?

It's as if your eyes demanded a fee for seeing, or your feet for walking. These parts of your body are formed for a specific purpose, and by working according to their inherent makeup come into their own. So too are we created by Nature to act benevolently, and when we have done something helpful or in some way conducive to the common interest, we have acted in harmony with our own inherent makeup, and also come into our own.

———— ✦ ————

THE CRUELTY OF ANGER

How cruel it is to forbid people from striving after what seems both advantageous and suitable to them! And, in a way, you do this when you get angry at their wrongdoing.

For they are certainly attracted to things because they think they're suitable and will be profitable.

"But it's not so."

Then you must teach them and show them rather than get so indignant.

———✦———

WHAT IS PROFITABLE?

Everything that happens to an individual is for the benefit of the whole: this should be enough.

But if you look closely you can also see this as a general rule: what is profitable to one person is also profitable to everyone. And let the word *profitable* be used here in its conventional sense, meaning things that are morally neutral, since whether you make a profit or a loss is not under the control of your will.

SOCIAL UNITY

Since you are an integral part of a social system, let every act of yours contribute to the harmonization of social life. Any action that is not related directly or remotely to this social aim disturbs your life, and destroys your unity.

CONCEPTIONS OF GOOD

When someone offends you, think at once about the conceptions they hold about good and evil.

For when you understand this, you'll pity them rather than be surprised or angry.

If you yourself consider the same things good that they do, it's your duty to pardon them. But if your conception of things that are good or evil are different, you'll still find it easier to be kind to those in error.

———•———

TOLERANCE

People were created for the sake of one another. Either teach them or bear with them.

———•———

ANGER AND STRESS

When you are annoyed at someone's mistake, immediately look at yourself and reflect how you also fail; for example, in thinking that good equals money, or pleasure, or a bit of fame.

By being mindful of this you'll quickly forget your anger, especially if you realize that the person was under stress, and could do little else. And, if you can, find a way to alleviate that stress.

LIFE AND DESTINY

Adapt yourself to the life you have been given; and truly love the people with whom destiny has surrounded you.

THE UNNATURAL LOOK

An angry look is absolutely unnatural. If it's constantly put on, the result is that all beauty dies, and eventually becomes completely extinguished and can never be lit up again.

Try to see from this very fact that it is against reason. For if we have lost even the consciousness of doing wrong, what reason can we find to carry on living?

❖

FORGETFULNESS

If you feel annoyed, you've forgotten that everything happens in obedience to universal Nature and that another person's stupidity has nothing to do with you.

You've also forgotten that things always happen, have always happened, and will happen again just like this, everywhere.

You've forgotten how close is the bond between an individual and the whole human race, for it's a community, not of a little blood or seed, but of mind; and each individual mind is a God, an emanation of the divine intelligence.

You've also forgotten that nothing belongs to us, but that our children and our bodies and our very souls come from that divine source. You've forgotten that everything depends on judgment.

And finally you've forgotten that every person lives only in the present moment, and can lose only this.

———— • ————

THE ERROR OF
THEIR WAYS

If someone is in error, instruct them kindly and show them where they have gone wrong. If this doesn't correct them, blame yourself, or better, blame no one.

———— • ————

THE BAD RETURN

When you have done a good deed that another has had the benefit of, why do you need a third reward—as fools do—praise for having done well or looking for a favor in return?

———————

THE FRUIT OF IGNORANCE

People who do wrong wrong themselves. People who act unjustly act unjustly to themselves, injuring their nature and making themselves evil.

———————

USELESS BLAME

If it's in your power to choose, what makes you do it? If it's in someone else's power, what do you blame? Chance? The gods? Both are ridiculous. You must blame no one.

If you can, you must correct the offender, and if you can't do this, at least correct the offense itself. If even this can't be done, what's the purpose of recriminations? For nothing should be done without a purpose.

------ • ------

REAL TIME

You don't have time to read.

But you do have time to restrain your arrogance; you have time to rise above pleasure and pain; to be superior to love of fame; and not to be annoyed by foolish and ungrateful people, but even to care for them.

------ • ------

BROTHERHOOD

It is a peculiarly human characteristic to love even those who do us wrong. This love is born when you recognize others as your brothers, who do wrong blindly, through ignorance.

Above all, you realize he's done you no real harm, for he hasn't made your mind any worse than it was before.

In any case both of you will soon be dead.

———◆———

THE VIRTUES OF FAMILY AND FRIENDS

When you want to cheer yourself up, think of the good qualities of those you live with. For instance, the energy of one, the modesty of another, the generosity of a third, and so on.

For nothing gives us as much pleasure as seeing the examples of the virtues presented in abundance by those who live among us. Therefore keep them always near at hand.

TALKING AND BEING

Stop talking about what the good person should be, and just be that person.

NEEDS AND RULES

Since you are part of and governed by Nature, observe and accept what your physical nature needs. Act on these needs, provided your living being does not become degraded by them.

Observe also what your individual nature

requires of you as a compassionate being. This you must also do provided your rational and social nature is not made worse by it.

If you use these rules, there is no need to worry about anything else.

THE COHERENT BODY

The body ought to be fit and composed, not agitated either in motion or in rest. We should require that the whole body exhibit the mind, as the face does when it maintains an expression of intelligence and symmetry. And all these must be maintained without posing.

THE ART OF WRESTLING

The art of living is more like wrestling than danc-
ing, in that we stand watchful and rooted to meet
whatever comes from unexpected directions.

FIRMNESS AND
GENTLENESS

Though people may try to stop you from following the correct path they can never divert you
from correct behavior. Just make sure they don't
force you to lose compassion toward them.

You need to be prepared for firm decisions
and action, without losing gentleness towards
those who obstruct or abuse you. It's as great a
weakness to be angry with them as it is to abandon your plan of action and give up through fear.
These are both like deserting soldiers: the one who

panics, as well as one alienated from his natural brothers and friends.

THE EYES ARE THE WINDOW OF THE SOUL

How empty and insincere is the person who says, "I've decided to be fair with you."

What nonsense! There's no need to say this. The intention will reveal itself, as if written on the forehead, or like an echo in the voice.

A person's character immediately shines in the eyes, just as one who is loved reads everything in the gaze of the beloved.

Sincerity and goodness should have their own unique smell, so that anyone who approaches has no choice but to recognize them at once.

The veneer of honesty is like a hidden razor. Nothing is more dangerous than the phony friendship of a wolf and this must be avoided.

Good, sincere, and kind people show their character in their faces for all to see.

DOING, NOT SAYING

A rational person is not changed for better or worse by their feelings but by their actions. So too do we judge excellence and failings by a person's behavior rather than their feelings.

THE BEST REVENGE

Not becoming like your enemy is the best revenge.

❦2❧

CULTIVATING
THE SELF

Moral Cultivation

The perfection of character consists in living each day as if it were the last and being neither violently excited, nor apathetic, nor insincere.

———•———

The Sage

Nature hasn't blended your mind so completely with your body, as to deny you the power of limiting yourself and bringing under your control everything that you are.

Always bear that in mind and, with it, remember how little is needed to live a happy life. Just because you've given up on becoming a great logician or a student of physics, don't despair of being free, modest, unselfish, and obedient to the will of God. It's quite possible to become a great sage and yet never be recognized.

———•———

THE PRINCIPLES

This will help remove your desire for empty fame: it's no longer in your power to live your whole life, or at least your mature life, in pursuit of philosophy; to yourself and to others it's clear that you fail as a philosopher. You're so muddled that it's not easy for you to gain that reputation, and the life of an Emperor mitigates against it.

Therefore, if you are truly aware of the situation, discard the thought "How do I look to others?" Be content if you can live the rest of your life as your nature demands. Consider what it wants, and let nothing else distract you; for you have experienced endless searching and not found happiness anywhere, not in logical thought, not in wealth, not in fame, not in self-indulgence—nowhere.

Then where can I find happiness? In doing what my nature requires. How can I do this? If I allow my impulses and actions to spring from my principles. What principles? They are about good and evil, that nothing is good for me that does not make me just, moderate, courageous, and independent; and nothing is evil that does not produce the exact opposite.

———— • ————

VITALITY OF THE MIND

Epicurus said, "When I was ill I didn't go on about my symptoms and ailments. Instead I continued to talk, as I always do, about the nature of things, and to the main point: how the mind, while conscious of all the infirmities of mere flesh, still remains undisturbed and preserves its own vitality. I didn't give the doctors a chance to put on airs, as if they were doing something great, but my life went on smoothly and happily."

You should do the same as Epicurus, in sickness and in all other trouble. Never to abandon philosophy no matter what happens to us is a principle of all the schools. Just be intent on what you are doing now and how you are doing it.

———— • ————

THE PLEASURE OF WISDOM

Don't be frustrated, discouraged, or impatient if you can't do everything according to your principles. If you fail, turn back satisfied that most of your actions follow man's good nature, and cherish the practice to which you return.

But don't return to your philosophy as if to a schoolmaster, but like someone with sore eyes who needs to apply a lotion. For this way it's easy to follow reason and find rest in it.

Philosophy demands the same things your own nature requires, but you seem to want something more. You seem to demand, "Why not even more pleasure?" But isn't this the very way pleasure deceives us? Surely generosity, freedom, simplicity, tranquillity, and reverence are enough?

For what can be more pleasant than wisdom itself, when you consider the safety and contentment of everything that relies on our mind's understanding and knowledge?

REASON AND VIRTUE

In the make-up of a reasonable person I find no virtue that opposes justice; but I see a virtue that opposes love of pleasure, and that is self-control.

LIVING UP TO NAMES

If you've given yourself these names: good, modest, true, rational, contented, and principled, then take care not to let others take their place. Should you lose them, quickly try to get them back.

Remember that the term rational implies a careful attention to every single thing without neglecting a detail; contentment lies in a willing acceptance of the things assigned to you by universal Nature; and principled is holding the thinking mind above the pleasurable and painful sensations of the flesh, above petty reputation, and death, and all such things.

If you can live up to these names, without wishing others to call you by them, you will become a changed man and will enter a new life. For to continue to live as you are, to be torn and soiled by your present way, shows the character of a fool who clings to life, like those gladiators half-eaten by lions. Though covered with wounds and gore, they still plead to be kept alive for one more day, though they will be flung again to the same claws and teeth.

Therefore ground yourself in the possession of these few names, and if you are able to live by them, live as if you had drifted to the islands of the blessed. But if you realize that they've escaped your grasp and you've lost them, go bravely into some corner of your mind where they may be sheltered, or even slip away at once from life, not in agitation, but with simplicity, freedom, and self-respect, having accomplished at least one admirable thing in your life: the way in which you left it.

To help recall these names, think of the gods and their wish not that we flatter them, but that every conscious being should become like them.

Remember too that the work of a fig tree is done by a fig tree, a dog does the work of a dog, a bee that of a bee, and so only a man can do the work of a man.

POINTS OF CONNECTION

You have three relationships: the first is to the body that envelopes you, the second is to the divine cause from which all things come; and the third is to those who live with you.

PRINCIPLES

Don't you see how experts will adapt themselves up to a point with amateurs, but still cling to the rules of their craft and not depart from them?

Isn't it deplorable that the architect and the doctor should have more respect for the principles of their own skills than man does for his reason, which he shares with the gods?

———•———

JUDGING APPEARANCES

Don't become rash or impetuous, but when an impulse stirs be concerned only about what is just. With each impression that forms, be certain you really grasp it.

———•———

TRUE KNOWLEDGE

Always take the direct route, because the direct route is the way of Nature; therefore say and do

everything with the soundest knowledge, for an
aim like this will free you from anxiety, and stress;
from all pretension and vanity.

———————————

THE ILLUSION
OF POSSESSIONS

A man shouldn't prize things that do not belong
inherently to mankind. They're not needed by a
man; for his nature doesn't promise them and isn't
fulfilled by them. Man's ultimate purpose doesn't
lie in things, and they don't represent the "good,"
which is the means to that end.

Besides, if any of these things did belong to a
man, it would then be wrong for him to despise
them and resist them. If these things were good,
then a man who showed contempt for them
wouldn't be worthy of praise, and if he failed to
take them for himself he wouldn't be considered
good, if they were "good."

The way it is, however, is that the more a man deprives himself, or even allows himself to be deprived, if he can calmly endure the loss, the better he becomes.

———◆———

KNOWING THE LIMIT

To seek the impossible is madness, but the foolish will always try.

———◆———

NURTURING YOURSELF WITH TRUTH

If anyone can show me, and convince me, that I have acted or thought in error, I will gladly change; for I seek the truth, and no one was ever injured by the truth. But a man injures himself if he lives with self-deception and ignorance.

————— • —————

CHANGE YOUR MIND

Always follow these two rules: first, act only on what your reasoning mind proposes for the good of humanity, and second, change your opinion if someone shows you it's wrong.

This change of mind must proceed only from the conviction that it's both correct and for the common good, but not because it will give you pleasure and make you popular.

————— • —————

THE WARRIOR SPIRIT

Don't waste the rest of your life thinking about other people, unless it's to help them in some way. For by wondering what so-and-so is getting up to, and why, and what he is saying or planning, you lose the chance to do something useful for yourself, and let your mind get clogged with thoughts like these.

We need to stop the mind from going on its aimless wanderings, specifically avoiding curiosity and malice. A rational mind should be so engaged that if someone should suddenly ask, "What are you thinking about?" you could with complete freedom and spontaneity say what was on your mind.

From your words it should be plain that everything about you is simple and kindly; that you are a sociable being who doesn't care to think about pleasure or sensual enjoyments at all; or to engage in competition, envy, or suspicion, or any other thoughts that would make you blush if you said you had them on your mind.

For such a man, who tries to live by the right values, becomes a priest and servant to the gods, using the spirit that is embedded within him, which makes him unsullied by pleasure, impervious to pain, untouched by insults, feeling no wrong; a warrior in the best fight, one who cannot be overcome by any desires, with a deep love of justice, and accepting with all his soul everything that happens to him as his great destiny.

Only rarely, and then out of necessity or for the common good, should he worry about what someone else thinks or says or does. For a man needs to cultivate himself, and he should be concerned with what he's been given out of the sum total of the universe; ensuring that his actions are correct and believing that what happens to him is for the best. For the spirit that's given to each man at birth goes with him and carries him along with it.

He needs to remember that all rational beings are his brothers, and although to care for your brother is innate in man's nature, he should only listen to those whose lives are really in accord with Nature.

For those who don't follow Nature's laws, he reminds himself about their characters both at home and abroad, by night and by day, and bears in mind the kind of company they keep.

So if these men praise him, he doesn't value their approval, since he knows they can hardly be satisfied with themselves.

———— • ————

No Time to Waste

Think about how many years you have been putting things off, and how often the gods have given you extra periods of grace, and still you don't use them.

It's about time you realized the nature of the universe of which you are a part, and the nature of the ruling power of the universe that has created you.

You have been given only a limited period of time, and if you do not use it for blowing away the clouds from your mind, it will pass away and you will go with it, never to return.

———— • ————

THE POWER OF THE MIND

In one way I feel very close to mankind, since I must respect other men and endure them. But when some of them block my good actions, then I feel an indifference toward man and consider him the same as I do the sun or the wind or a wild animal.

Now it's true that these may also impede my actions, but they don't frustrate my will and temperament, which have the power of altering existing conditions; for the mind can transform every obstacle into something new, purposeful, and creative to help us on the way.

———— • ————

THE SILENT JUDGE

For you, evil does not come from the mind of someone else or from any changes to your body. Where does it come from then? It is your mind that makes judgments about good and evil. Stop these judgments and all will be well.

And even if its neighbour, your poor body, is sliced, burned, ruptured or blemished, still let that judge stay silent. Let your mind pronounce nothing to be either good or evil if it can happen equally to both good men and bad. For anything that can happen equally to one who lives against Nature, and one who lives in harmony with it, is neither helpful to Nature nor contrary to it.

———◆———

CLENCHED FISTS

When using your principles emulate the boxer, not the gladiator. For the gladiator must pick up and lay down his sword, but the boxer always has his hands, and only needs to clench them.

———•———

SURVIVAL BY SIMPLICITY

Don't disturb yourself by ruminating on your entire life; don't dwell on the many troubles that may happen to you. On each occasion ask yourself, "What is there in this thought that is unendurable and unbearable?"

For you'll be ashamed to admit that it can all be endured. Then remember: the past and future can't harm you—and only the present can. And this can be reduced to very little, if you only limit it, and your mind would be very weak if it couldn't endure even this.

———•———

SELF-JUDGMENT

I am often amazed that even though every man loves himself most of all, he values his own judgment of himself less than the opinion of others.

So if a wise teacher appeared and asked a man never to think or plan anything that couldn't immediately be talked about, no one could stand it for a single day.

Sadly, we have more regard for our neighbors' judgment than for our own.

———•———

THE JUDGES

Penetrate into someone's leading principles, and you will see the judges you fear, and what poor judges they are of themselves.

———•———

AIM AND PURPOSE

"The person who does not have one steady and unvarying aim in life, cannot be the same person all through that life."

But this saying is incomplete unless you add what this one aim should be. The majority of people have varying opinions about all the things that they think of as good, but only agree on those few things that concern the welfare of society.

In the same way we should propose to ourselves a steady and unvarying aim of a communal kind. For those who direct all their efforts to this aim, will unify all their actions, and become coherent with themselves.

———————

THE FOUR DEVIATIONS

There are four deviations of the mind to constantly guard against, and once found, to abolish by saying:

This thought is unnecessary.

This one tends to destroy community.

What you're about to say doesn't come from your true self (for you should consider it completely absurd if you don't speak from your heart).

The fourth is when you reproach yourself, for this is evidence of your inner spirit being overcome and giving in to your lower, mortal part, the body and its gross pleasures.

ACTION AND INTENTION

Make it a practice when something is done, no matter by who, to ask yourself, "What is their intention in doing this?"

But start with yourself; examine yourself first.

THE RULING MIND

Whatever it is that I am, it is a little flesh, a little breath, and the ruling mind.

Throw away your books; stop distracting yourself: it's forbidden. As if you were on the road to death, despise the flesh for it is blood and bones and a network, a complex of nerves, veins, and arteries. And the breath too, what is it? Air, and not always the same air, but every moment sent out and again sucked in.

Concentrate on the mind, your ruler: you are old; it's time to stop your mind acting like a slave, pulled puppet-like by the strings of selfish desires.

Stop fuming at your destiny by grumbling about today and shrinking from the future.

———————

ASHES AND SMOKE

How does the ruling mind make use of itself? For everything depends on this, and everything else, whether it is in the power of your will or not, is only lifeless ashes and smoke.

NO REGRETS

Regret is a kind of remorse for having let something useful go by; but the good is always useful, and a sage would look after it. Now a sage would never regret having let a pleasure go by. Pleasure then is neither good nor useful.

GODLIKE TOLERANCE

The gods, though they live forever, do not resent having to eternally tolerate mankind, when many of them are so often worthless; in fact, they must care for them in all kinds of ways.

And you, destined as you are to vanish soon, are you washing your hands of them, even though you are one of the culprits?

———◆———

PROBLEM SOLVING

Today I have removed myself from my problems, or rather have gotten rid of my problems; for they weren't outside me, but inside and especially in the judgments of my mind.

———◆———

UNIMPULSIVE

If it's not right, don't do it: if it's not true, don't say it. Keep your impulses in reserve.

———◆———

CONCENTRATION

Stop fantasizing! Don't be a puppet on the strings of impulse! Stay here in the present. Recognize what is really happening to you. Divide and separate every object into its causes or its matter. Think about your last breaths on earth. Let the wrong that was done by any person remain with that person.

———◆———

Self-Control

Dissolve fantasies: check desire: extinguish cravings: let your governing self retain her power.

The Power of Clarity

Erase your idle fantasies by saying to yourself, "It is in my power not to allow evil into my soul; to keep out any desire or disturbance, since by looking I can see into the nature of all things and use each according to its worth."

Remember, this power is a gift from nature.

DECONSTRUCTION

Observe closely everything that makes an impression on your mind, and deconstruct it by separation into causes, matter, purpose, and the time when it must cease.

———— • ————

PERFECT SECURITY

If you remove your judgment about what makes you suffer, your self stands rooted in perfect security.

"Who is this self?"

It is reason.

"But I'm not reason!"

OK. Then don't let reason itself cause you trouble. If any other part of you suffers, let it form its own judgment about itself.

———— • ————

DISCERNMENT

Value your power of judgment.

By it alone does your mind know if your opinions are at odds with Nature, or contrary to the character of a rational being.

And this power promises freedom from self-deception, friendliness with others, and harmony with the will of heaven.

———◆———

LIMIT YOUR JUDGMENT

If you suppose that anything beyond your will is either good or evil, it follows that if evil happens to you, or you lose a good thing, you will blame the gods, and hate those who caused the misfortune, or whom you suspect of being the cause.

Indeed, we do many injustices because we fail to regard things beyond our will as morally neutral. But if we limit our judgment of good and evil only to those things that our will controls, there is no reason either for finding fault with God or maintaining a hostile attitude to man.

———•———

❧ 3 ❧

THE
INNER
SPIRIT

❋

THE INNER SPIRIT

God sees the inner spirit stripped of flesh, skin, and all debris. For his own mind only touches the spirit that he has allowed to flow from himself into our bodies.

And if you can act in the same way, you will rid yourself of all suffering. For surely if you are not preoccupied with the body that encloses you, you will not trouble yourself about clothes, houses, fame, and other showy trappings.

———•———

THE WELL

Dig inside; inside is the fountain of good, and it will forever flow, if you will forever dig.

———•———

THE FORTRESS
OF THE MIND

Remember that your governing self becomes invincible when it draws into itself, and calmly refuses to act against its will, even if its resistance may sometimes seem irrational.

Think how much stronger it will be when it deliberately uses reason and judgment to form a decision. For the mind freed from passions is like a fortress, and there is nothing more secure in which to retreat and find unceasing sanctuary.

Those who haven't yet seen this are ignorant; but those who have seen it, and still don't seek its shelter, are unfortunate indeed.

DEVELOPING SPIRIT

When your inner spirit is in harmony with Nature it can adapt easily to all events and possibilities.

For this spirit does not need any special matter or substance to function, but works on whatever obstacles are put in its way.

We can compare it to a bonfire that consumes whatever is thrown in it: if the fire is feeble it can be extinguished, but a strong blaze feeds on everything, and its flames grow ever higher.

PEACE LIES WITHIN

Nothing is sadder than people who go around all of creation and, as the poet says, "search the bowels of the earth" and peer intently into the minds of others without once realizing that all they need to discover is their own inner spirit and to nurture it sincerely.

Such nurturing consists of keeping it free from desires and negligence, and from feeling dissatisfaction with the ways of God and men.

For we should be awestruck by the beauty of

creation and compassionate toward all humanity,
our brothers. And even when we feel pity for
another's ignorance of good and evil, we should be
aware that this is like a blind man being unable to
tell black from white.

INNER TRUTH

Whatever anyone else says or does, I must be true
to myself, just as if gold or emerald or the color
purple would say, "Whatever anyone may do or
say, I must be an emerald and keep my color."

THE HIGHEST POWER

In the universe, respect the highest power, namely
the creative force that directs and makes use of all

things. In the same way, you must respect the highest power in yourself, for it is of the same creative kind.

For this is what makes use of the rest of you, and directs your life.

———— • ————

A MOBILE HOME
FOR THE SOUL

"Sweep me up and send me where you please."

For there I will retain my spirit, tranquil and content, as long as it can feel and act in harmony with its own nature.

Is a change of place enough reason for my soul to become unhappy and worn, for me to become depressed, humbled, cowering, and afraid? Can you discover any reasons for this?

———— • ————

THE HIDDEN POWER

Remember that our buttons are pushed by what is hidden deep inside: there lies the power of persuasion; there lies life; there, if one may say so, lies the very self.

In contemplating your true self, don't include the body that surrounds you and the limbs attached to it. They are like tools, the only difference being that they grow from the body.

Without the mind that moves and restrains them, there is no more activity in these limbs than in the potter's wheel, the writer's pen, or the carpenter's ax.

READINESS

How can I cultivate a soul that, if right now it had to be separated from my body, is equally ready to face extinction, dissolution, or continued existence?

This readiness can only come from my own decision, found from reflection and carried out with a dignity able to influence others, without making a drama out of it.

———— • ————

THE INVIOLATE SOUL

Pain is either an evil to the body—in which case let the body speak for itself—or to the soul.

But it is in the soul's power to maintain its own serenity and tranquillity and not to consider pain as an evil.

For every judgment, impulse, desire, and aversion comes from deep inside, where nothing evil can reach it.

———— • ————

QUALITIES OF SOUL

These are the properties of a rational soul: It is self-reflective, self-analytical, and self-sufficient; the fruit it produces is for its own enjoyment (unlike the fruit produced by plants and even animals, which others enjoy).

It is always complete, wherever life may reach its limit. Unlike a dance or a play, which, if interrupted, is incomplete, the soul, in all of life's moments and whenever it's finally stopped, makes what it has produced so whole and complete that it can truly say, "I have what is mine."

The soul can expand to contain the entire universe and the surrounding void. Seeing its own formless form, it extends itself into the infinity of time, embracing and comprehending the continuous renewal of creation.

It knows that future generations will see nothing new, even as our ancestors saw nothing greater than we see today. In a sense, any forty-year-old with some understanding has seen everything that has been and will be because of the similarity of all happenings.

Other qualities of a rational soul include love of one's neighbor, truthfulness and modesty, and valuing nothing greater than itself. Since this last quality is also a property of law, the principle of rationality and the principle of justice are one and the same.

———— • ————

THE SPIRIT OF GOD AND MAN

Live with the gods.

Those who live with the gods always show their souls to be satisfied with the life assigned to them. They constantly follow the dictates of their spirit, the same spirit that Zeus has given to each one of us as a guardian and guide.

And this spirit is our mind and reason.

———— • ————

QUESTIONS FOR
THE SOUL

Will you, my soul, one day become good, simple, unified, and open; more apparent than my surrounding body? Will you ever taste the sweetness of a loving affectionate nature? Can you become complete and without desires, longing for nothing, not craving anything living or nonliving for your pleasures? Will you never stop wanting still more time to enjoy them, in a beautiful place with a mild climate, surrounded by a harmonious society? Can you be satisfied with the present, pleased with your situation, able to convince yourself that you have everything you need and that it all comes from the gods?

Life is fine for you, and whatever it pleases the gods to give is good. The nourishment they provide for a perfect living oneness—so good, just, and beautiful—gives life, binds together, contains and embraces all things which at their dissolution return to their source for the creation of new life.

Will you, my soul, ever live in community

with gods and men without finding fault with them, and not be condemned by them in turn?

———— • ————

THE AUTONOMOUS SOUL

External things cannot touch the soul, not one bit; they have no way to get into it, and no power to sway or move it. The soul sways and moves by itself, and when things present themselves to it, it responds to them by its own standards and judges them accordingly.

———— • ————

DAMAGING THE SOUL

The human soul damages itself when it becomes (as far as it is able) a kind of cancerous tumor on the Universe.

For to lose our harmony through tedious activity puts us in opposition to Nature—the same Nature that runs through each of us.

And when in anger we reject other people, or turn on them with the aim of inflicting pain, we damage our souls even more.

A third way is when we surrender to pleasure or pain. A fourth, when we are insincere or lie. A fifth when we act thoughtlessly or aimlessly, wasting our energies, since even the smallest acts need to be done with some purpose in mind.

And for intelligent creatures, that purpose must be to follow the reason and law of the world itself.

THE ILLUMINATED SOUL

The sphere of the soul maintains its perfect form when it is not extended toward any object, or shrinking in on itself, or dispersed or sunk down, but only when it is bathed in light, the light in which it sees the truth, both in all things and in itself.

———————

LIVING THE GOOD LIFE

How to live the good life? The ability is in your soul, as long as it remains unattached to things that are morally neutral to it.

And the soul will remain unattached if it carefully scrutinizes each of these neutral things both as a whole, and by separation into the elements that compose them.

Remember that none of these things are responsible for creating our conception about them; these things are motionless and so can't even approach us. It is we ourselves who create ideas about things, and, as we might say, drag them inside ourselves. It is in our power not to include them, and even if these conceptions have unconsciously gained admission to our minds, to erase them.

Remember too that you only have a short time left to give attention like this, and then life will be at an end. Besides, how much difficulty is there in doing all this?

For if these things are in harmony with Nature, rejoice in them, and you will find them easy. If not, then look for harmony with your own nature, and strive toward this, even if it brings no glory; for every man is justified in seeking his own good.

———•———

FUTILITY OF ISOLATION

If you've ever seen a dismembered hand, foot, or a head lying by itself apart from its body, you have an idea of what it feels like when you refuse to accept your destiny, cutting yourself off from others or acting selfishly.

You feel that you've become an outcast from

the oneness of Nature—for you were born a part of Nature but have cut yourself off. Yet even at this late stage there's a beautiful remedy; it's still in your power to become part of this oneness. No other part of Nature, after it's been separated and cut off, is allowed by God to reunite.

Then consider God's supreme kindness that has put it within our power not to be broken off at all from the whole. And even if separation does happen, the gift of God allows complete integration with that oneness and resumption of our given place.

———— ◆ ————

ADAPTATION AND INTEGRITY

Every separate action furthers the integrity of your life, and you must be content if every act succeeds as well as it can. No one can stop you from achieving this aim.

"Perhaps some obstacle may get in the way."

Still this should not stop you from acting fairly, moderately, and considerately.

"Perhaps I will lose the power to act."

If you can accept that disability and are willing to adapt your efforts to your other abilities, another opportunity will immediately present itself, and it will be one that will naturally adapt itself to the integrity you seek.

GOOD VISION

Observe carefully and you will see that everything that happens happens for a purpose.

. I don't just mean the actual unfolding of events in time, but the way these events carry meaning, as if some guiding hand were giving each event its own significance.

Continue to observe yourself, and follow this same principle: that all your actions must be good—*good* meaning the correct way a man should act.

Express this goodness in everything you do.

SELFLESSNESS

Experience the pleasure of moving from one service to the community to another, thinking always of God.

DIFFERENT STROKES

Be generous and open with animals and objects, since you have reason and they have none. But toward human beings, who share your reason, behave in a neighborly way.

Always call on the gods for help, and do not

concern yourself about how long you spend doing this; for even three hours spent like this is sufficient.

———————◆·◆———————

NICE WORK IF YOU CAN GET IT

If any work is done in harmony with the inner spirit that we share with the gods, there's nothing to fear; for when we can obtain benefit from work that moves on an easy path and obeys the laws of our being, we should not expect to come to harm.

———————◆·◆———————

THE UNIVERSAL MIND

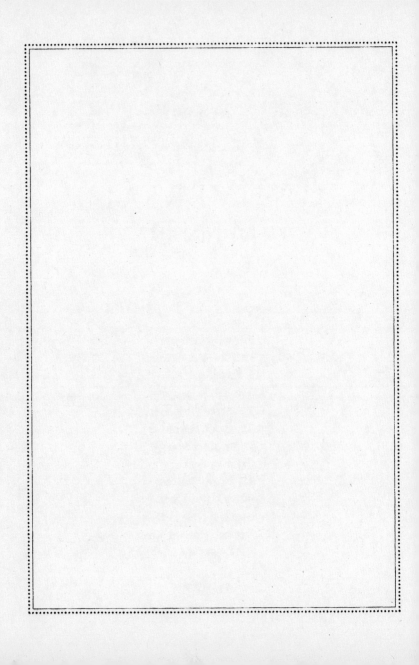

ABSOLUTE UNITY

All things are linked with one another, and this oneness is sacred; there is nothing that is not inter-connected with everything else. For things are interdependent, and they combine to form this universal order.

There is only one universe made up of all things, and one creator who pervades them; there is one substance and one law, namely, common reason in all thinking creatures, and all truth is one—if, as we believe, there is only one path of perfection for all beings who share the same mind.

THE UNIVERSE OF MIND

No longer breathe only with the atmosphere sur-rounding you, but let your mind breathe in a similar way with the mind that runs through everything.

For the power of mind is as universal and pervasive to the person willing to draw it in, as is the power of air to the person able to breathe.

———•———

FIRST IMPRESSIONS

Say nothing more to yourself than your first impressions report. Suppose you hear that someone is speaking badly of you. This has been reported to you, but you haven't heard that your reputation has been injured.

I see that my child is ill. This I do see; that she is in danger I don't see, but create my own fears.

So always stay with first impressions. Add nothing from your own feelings, and you will be safe. Or rather, add just one thought about the great universal Nature that brings all things to fulfillment.

———•———

THE THREE PRINCIPLES

Don't look around and speculate about other men's inner selves. Go straight on where nature leads you, both Universal Nature, through what happens to you, and your own nature in terms of how you should act. Every being needs to act according to its own nature; and, in the same way that all created things are made for the sake of rational beings (following the general law that the inferior have been created for the superior), so all rational beings are created only for one another's sake.

The first principle of human nature is our social need.

The second is not to yield to the impulses of the body, for it is the property of reason and the intellect to limit itself, and not be overpowered by either the senses or impulses, which are the animal in us. The mind claims superiority and does not permit itself to be overpowered by the others; and with good reason, for it is formed by Nature to use all of them.

The third principle for the rational being is freedom from error and from deception.

Let the guiding self, reason, hold fast to these principles and go straight ahead, and it will possess what is its own.

THE STOIC PHILOSOPHY

You can only be happy by being correct, and to be correct is to be kind to your own kind; to rise above the impulses of the senses; to form a true judgment of the world of appearances; and to study the nature of the universe and its great works.

DIGESTING OBSTACLES

Nature has given to each conscious being every power she possesses, and one of these abilities is this: just as Nature converts and alters every obstacle and opposition, and fits them into their predestined place, making them a part of herself, so too the rational person is able to finesse every obstacle into an opportunity, and to use it for whatever purpose it may suit.

———— •———

REASON KNOWS

Universal Reason, which governs everything, knows its own characteristics, and what it creates, and the material on which it works.

———— •———

THE CREATIVE FORCE OF REASON

Matter in the universe is flexible and compliant; and reason, which governs it, has in itself no motive for doing evil, for it is not malicious, and so does not cause evil or harm to anything.

Yet all things are born, nurtured, and perfected through this principle.

PROTEAN REASON

The guiding principle of Reason is both self-starting and self-directed. Not only does it create itself into whatever it wants, it makes everything that happens to it also appear to be of whatever kind it wants.

SELECTIVE VISION

The healthy eye should see everything visible and not say, "I only want to see green things"; for this is the condition of a diseased eye. The healthy ear and nose should sense everything that can be heard and smelled. A healthy stomach should consume all food, just like a millstone that crushes every grain it has been made to grind.

In the same way, a healthy mind should be prepared for every circumstance. But someone who says, "Let my lovely children live, and make all men praise whatever I do," is like an eye that only likes green, or teeth that want to chew only the soft and pliable.

EVERYTHING HAS A PLACE

The Universal mind is a social mind. This is why it has made the inferior for the sake of the superior, and then connected the higher together. You see how it makes some play a supporting role, then coordinates and assigns to everything its proper share, and the best things are unified in a harmonious rapport.

———— • ————

ATTENTION TO THE MIND

Hurry to examine your mind, and compare it to your neighbor's and to the Universe: your own so that you can make it just; that of your neighbor, so that you can see that his mind is the same as yours; knowing this, you can judge whether it's informed by ignorance or knowledge.

That of the Universe so that you can remember the whole of which you are but a speck.

———— • ————

FREE WILL

Remember that to change your mind and to follow someone who corrects your error is not to be less free. For this change is your own, an action taken according to your own desire, judgment, and understanding.

———— ◆ ————

✕5✕

CONTEMPLATING DEATH

FACING DEATH

The person who fears death either fears the total loss of all consciousness or the onset of new sensations. But if you have no consciousness, you will not feel any pain, and if you acquire new sensations, you will just be a different kind of living creature and so will not cease to live.

THE MIND'S EYE

Our mind observes how swiftly all things vanish away. In space all bodies decay and in time even their memory fades.

We should also consider the nature of all objects of sense—especially those that attract with the seduction of pleasure, the threat of pain, or the call of fame. How cheap, contemptible, and sordid they are and how quickly they perish and die—all this is the job of the mind to observe.

We should also consider the value of the people whose words and opinions assign praise and blame. We need to look at the nature of death, and look at it objectively without the emotional baggage we carry about it. We will then find it to be merely a process of Nature. And anyone afraid of a process of Nature is a child.

Our mind by such observation can discover how we are in contact with God, which part of us maintains that contact, and what conditions are necessary to make this possible.

———————

PRECIOUS MOMENT

Consider this: every day that wastes away leaves one less day to live. Even if we live longer, there is no guarantee that our minds will avoid senility and so lose the ability to acquire both human and spiritual knowledge.

For if a man falls into senility, breathing and eating, dreaming and lust and everything else carry on. But the ability to make full use of the mind, and to assess correctly the demands of duty, to clearly make distinctions between things and to decide if he is ready to depart this life, and everything else that relies on a man's applied intelligence, all this is already gone.

We need to hurry, then, not only because every day brings us nearer to death, but because our conception and understanding of things may deteriorate first.

The Vanity of Fame

Words that were once current, and names that were once famous are now old and dim. For all things soon fade into fable and complete oblivion buries them.

And this is true for even those whose lives glittered like stars. For most of us, as soon as we have breathed our last, we are gone and no one speaks of us. What is eternal fame? Complete vanity.

Then what should we concern ourselves with? Only with this: correct thoughts, unselfish acts, and words that never lie. We need to keep a disposition that gladly accepts everything that happens as necessary, familiar, and flowing from the original source.

IN PERSPECTIVE

Discard everything except these few truths: we can live only in the present moment, in this brief now; all the rest of our life is dead and buried or shrouded in uncertainty. Short is the life we lead, and small our patch of earth.

And just as petty is the greatest fame, kept

alive in the memories of others, who will themselves soon die; of what value is the memory of
those who don't even know their own selves,
much less one who died ages ago?

READY FOR DEPARTURE

Everything you wish to eventually achieve, you
can have right now, if you don't refuse it to yourself. And this means taking no notice of the past,
trusting the future to providence, and living now
in union with faith and justice.

In union with faith so that you may be content with whatever destiny brings, for Nature
designed it for you and you for it. In union with
justice, so that you may always freely and frankly
speak the truth, and act with respect for the law
and the rights of every person.

Don't be hampered by anyone's malicious

thoughts or slander; or by the sensations of the poor flesh that has grown about you, for your body can look after itself.

So when the time approaches for you to make your departure, forgetting everything else, you should value only your ruling mind and the spirit within. If you can lose the fear of death and replace it with the fear that you have not even begun to live in harmony with Nature—then you can become worthy of the universe that has produced you, and you will cease to be a stranger in your own land, bewildered by daily events as if they were somehow unexpected, and dependent on outside things.

INSIDE OUT

People's actions follow an inner need. If you refuse to accept this, then you won't allow the fig tree to yield its juice.

But bear this in mind: within a very short time both you and everyone you know will be dead.

And soon not even your names will be remembered.

———————

Seizing the Day

Constantly remind yourself of the doctors, now dead, who worried over the sick; of the astrologers who prophesied the deaths of others; of the many philosophers and their endless discourses on death and immortality; the great heroes who slaughtered thousands; the tyrants who abused their power over men's lives with such insolence as if they were gods; and many cities that are buried like Babylon, Pompeii, and countless others.

Add to this list all the men you have known; how one man buries another, only to be laid out dead himself, and a third buries him; and all this in a twinkling.

This is it: the parade of humanity is transient and trivial, and what was yesterday a little mucus, tomorrow will be a mummy or ashes. Pass your brief time conforming to Nature, and finish your journey in contentment, just as the olive falls when it is ready, blessing nature that produced it, and thanking the tree that gave it life.

SLAVE AND MASTER

Hippocrates could cure the sick but could not heal himself. The Chaldean astrologers foretold many deaths, until fate caught up with them. Alexander the Great, Pompey, and Julius Caesar, after decimating whole cities, and cutting to shreds in combat tens of thousands of men and horses, also came to their last hour. Vermin killed Democritus, and vermin of another kind destroyed Socrates.

So what's the moral? Just this: You went on board, you set sail, and you've made it to port.

Step ashore: if to a second life, then no doubt the gods will be there to greet you. But if you disembark to unconsciousness, you will cease to suffer from pains and pleasures and slavery to your body, which in any case is far inferior to its master.

For the mind is intelligence and spirit, but the body is earth and corruption.

———•———

HOW TO LIVE

Soon, very soon, you will be ashes, or a skeleton and just a name or not even a name, for what is a name but just sound and echo? And to pursue the things we prize in life, which are empty, rotten, and trifling, we become like little dogs biting one another, or children bickering or laughing and then immediately crying.

Because faith, modesty, justice, and truth are fled, "Up to Olympus from the spacious earth."

Why then keep on going, if the objects of

sense are in constant flux and never stand still, and the doors of perception are easily clouded and give false impressions, and the poor soul itself is just an exhalation of the blood? To have a good name in a world like this is meaningless. Why not just sit in tranquillity and wait for the end, whether it's extinction or transformation?

And until that time comes, what do you need? Why, what else than to worship and bless the gods, to do good toward your fellow men, and to practice tolerance and self-restraint? And as for everything that is beyond the limits of your poor flesh and breath, remember that this is not yours and is not within your power.

———◆———

LIVING IN
THE PRESENT

If you are doing what is right, it should make no difference to you if you are freezing or warm, drowsy or well rested, being praised or blamed, and either dying or doing something else.

For even the act by which we die is one of the acts of life, and so it's important that even at the moment of death we make the best use of the present.

———— • ————

THE GREAT LEVELER

Death brought Alexander the Great and his stable boy together; for they were either received by the same life-giving principles of the Universe, or they were both scattered equally among the atoms.

———— • ————

THE LEGACY
OF DEATH

Death releases us from sense impressions, from the impulses of our hungers, the wayward wandering of our thoughts, and the need to care for the body.

———•———

THE LIVING CORPSE

Think of yourself today as a dead man, as one whose life is now finished; and with that in mind, live out what further time you are given in complete harmony with Nature.

———•———

WAITING FOR LIFE,
WAITING FOR DEATH

Do not fear death, but welcome it, since it too comes from Nature. For just as we are young and grow old, and flourish and reach maturity, have teeth and a beard and gray hairs, conceive, become pregnant and bring forth new life, and all the other natural processes that follow the seasons of our existence, so also do we have death.

A thoughtful man will never take death lightly, impatiently, or scornfully, but will wait for it as one of life's natural processes.

As you now wait for the time when your child shall emerge from your wife's womb, so be ready for the hour when your soul will emerge from its shell.

If your heart needs a basic kind of comfort, you can accept death most easily by observing the environment you will be taken from, and the morals of the characters your soul will no longer have to mingle with. For although it's not right to be so annoyed with them, it's still your duty to care for them and to bear with them gently. Don't forget that your departure will be from men who don't share your principles.

For this is the only thing, if there is one, that could drag us against the tide and make us cling to life, to be able to live among like-minded people. But when you contemplate the weariness of living with discontented people, you say, "Come quickly, death, for fear I, too, shall forget how to live."

A MOMENT IN TIME

All that you see will rapidly pass away, and those who gaze at the world await their own passing in time, so is there really so great a difference between an aged grandmother and the baby who dies in its cradle?

DEATH IS
NOT TERRIBLE

When a man finds his complete satisfaction in everything that each hour brings him; when he does not care if his actions are many or few, so long as they accord with strict reason; when it does not matter to him whether his stay in this world is long or fleeting—then not even death itself can be a thing of terror for him.

The man who considers the good to be that which comes in due season, and who thinks it doesn't matter whether he has done more or fewer acts that are in accord with Nature, and to whom it makes no difference whether he contemplates the world for a longer or a shorter time—for a man like this death is not a terrible thing.

———————

CONTEMPLATION OF LIFE AND DEATH

Contemplate what state the human body and soul should be in when overtaken by death; and consider the brevity of life, the inconceivable abyss of time past and time future, the passivity of all matter.

NOT INDISPENSABLE

Even if your heart should burst, the world will carry on just as before.

SELF-RESPECT

Don't seek to gain anything for yourself that forces you to break your word or lose self-respect; to hate, suspect, or curse another; or to be insincere or to desire something that needs to remain secret.

Look to the man whose main desire is to nurture his mind and his inner spirit. He does not fuss, complain, or crave either solitude or a crowd. And, most important of all, he will live without either striving or avoiding, and will not care whether his life is long or short.

If death comes for him at this very instant, he will go as easily as if he were doing any other act needing self-respect and calm, being careful of only this through his life: that his thoughts do not stray into paths incompatible with an intelligent and social being.

———————

DEPRIVED BY DEATH

Every time you do something, pause and ask yourself, "Do I find death so dreadful because it will deprive me of this activity?"

THE INCOMPLETE PLAN

How can the gods, after having arranged everything so carefully and lovingly for mankind, have overlooked only one thing: that some really fine people, who through good acts and dedicated practice have come very close to the Godhead, should be completely extinguished once they die, never to be reborn?

If this is their fate, rest assured that if there was need for a different plan, the gods would have made it. For any plan that's fair would also be possible; and if that plan were in accord with Nature, Nature would have made it happen.

NURTURING SPIRIT

Body, soul, and mind. To the body belongs sensation, to the soul desire, and to the mind principle. We share with bears and tigers the world of sense impressions, and to be swayed by waves of desire belongs both to wild beasts and to degenerates. The same mind that enlightens us to our duty inhabits those who deny the gods, are traitors, and perform vile acts behind locked doors.

If all of this is common to all, there remains only one unique gift for the good man: to welcome everything that happens as destiny unfolds. Not to pollute his inner spirit or disturb it with a jumble of images, but to keep it tranquil and nurture it, obeying that inner presence as if it were holy, clinging to the truth and acting justly.

And if skeptics doubt that the good man lives a simple, modest, and contented life, he is not angry with them but does not deviate from his path, since a man needs to come to the finish line pure and peaceful, ready to depart, at one with the Universe.

Sensible Living

In the life of man, his time is but an instant, his substance ceaselessly changing, his senses degraded, the flesh of his body subject to decay, his soul turbulent, his fortune difficult to predict, and his fame a question mark. In a word, his body is like a rushing stream, his soul an insubstantial dream, life is warfare, he is a stranger in a foreign land, and even after fame comes oblivion.

How can a man find a sensible way to live? One way and one only—philosophy. And my philosophy means keeping that vital spark within you free from damage and degradation, using it to transcend pain and pleasure, doing everything with a purpose, avoiding lies and hypocrisy, not relying on another person's actions or failings. To accept everything that comes, and everything that is given, as coming from that same spiritual source.

So when death comes for me I shall meet it with a cheerful mind. Since no harm comes to the elements when they continuously change from one to the other, why should I be afraid about the change and dissolution of my own elements? For this is the way of Nature, and nothing is evil that comes from Nature.

———— ◆ ————

THE PLAYMAKER

Marcus, you have been a citizen of this great world community; what difference does it make if it's for five years or fifty? Whatever is consistent with its laws is fair for everyone.

Why is it a raw deal if it's not a dictator or a warped judge who sends you away from this state, but the same Nature that brought you into it?

It's the same as if a producer who employed an actor banned him from the stage:

"But I haven't finished all five acts yet, only three of them."

Exactly, but in this particular life these three acts are the whole drama; for the complete play is determined by the one who was the cause of its composition, and now of its dissolution—and that's not you.

Leave the stage satisfied, for she who releases you is also satisfied.

———✦———

❧6❧

EVERYTHING
CHANGES

Swept Away

Time is a river flowing with the elements of creations; and a violent torrent, for as soon as a thing appears, it is swept away, and instantly replaced by another, which in turn is itself swept away.

Fleeting Life

Some things rush into existence, and others hasten out of it; and of those coming into life some part is already extinct.

Movement and flux are continually renewing the world, just as the unbroken course of time makes eternity forever young. In this flowing river, on which no one can stand, what is there for us to value among the things rushing by? It would be like a man falling in love with a passing sparrow, which is already out of sight.

Surely a man's life is as fleeting as the vaporization of the soul from his blood or his breath inhaled from the air? For just as you draw in a single breath and then return it, which you do in every moment, so you will have to return the actual power of breathing, which you had originally at your birth, to the source from which it came.

METAMORPHOSIS

When something dies it does not disappear from the universe. If it stays on earth, it changes and is dissolved into its separate particles, which are the elements that form the universe and yourself.

These elements also undergo change, but they don't complain about it.

THE NATURE OF CHANGE

Why should anyone be afraid of change? What can take place without it? What can be more pleasing or more suitable to universal Nature?

Can you take your bath without the firewood undergoing a change? Can you eat, without the food undergoing a change? And can anything useful be done without change?

Don't you see that for you to change is just the same, and is equally necessary for universal Nature?

———— ✦ ————

LIVING IN THE PRESENT

Remember that even if you were to live for three thousand years, or thirty thousand, you could not lose any other life than the one you have, and there will be no other life after it. So the longest and the shortest lives are the same.

For this present moment is shared by all living creatures, but the time that is past is gone forever. No one can lose the past or the future, for if they don't belong to you, how can they be taken from you?

Keep in mind these two things: first, that since the beginning of time the cycles of creation have shown the same recurring patterns, so it makes no difference if you live for one hundred years, two hundred years, or forever. Second, that the person who lives the longest life and the one who lives the shortest lose exactly the same thing.

For the present moment is the only thing you can take from anyone, since this is all they really own. No one can lose what they do not own.

SAME OLD STORY

All things are the same: common in experience, ephemeral in time, and worthless in material. Everything now is just as it was in the time of those long buried and gone.

———————◆———————

THE BIG PICTURE

You have within you the power to obliterate many superfluous and disturbing things, for they are entirely in your mind.

In the inner space this creates you can comprehend the whole universe, contemplate the eternity of time, and observe the driving pace of change: how short the time from birth to death, compared with the endless aeons before and the infinity that follows.

———————◆———————

LIVING ABOVE
TURMOIL

I often consider the speed with which things sweep past us and disappear, both things that exist in Nature and those just coming into existence. For life is like a river in continual flow, its actions moving in constant change, its causes weaving in infinite variety; nothing standing still.

And I also think about things near at hand, this endless abyss of the past and future that spreads out from me and into which all things disappear. A man is a fool if he gets puffed up with these things, or dwells on them and makes himself miserable. For they will bother him only for a moment, and then they vanish.

———— • ————

VITAL CHANGE

Observe how all things are created by change, and consider how Nature likes nothing better than to change existing things and create new things just like them.

For everything that exists is in a sense the seed of what will emerge from it.

But remember not to limit your idea of seeds to the ones planted in the earth or womb, which are only the most obvious examples.

CHANGE IS NEUTRAL

If it's not an "evil" for things to undergo change, then it can't be a "good" for things to be the result of change.

TRANSMUTATION

All material things swiftly change; if we presume
that all matter is one, then they will become vapor.
Otherwise they will disperse into their atoms.

———— • ————

AT HOME IN
THE UNIVERSE

Reality appears to be so illusory as to be almost
incomprehensible, even to philosophers like the
Stoics. Our perceptions are relative and changeable, and who has ever met a man who has never
changed his views?

Look, then, at the material objects of life,
and consider how trivial and short-lived they are,
and how often they are owned by scoundrels and
thieves. Should you look at the characters of those
you live with, it is hardly possible to endure even
the best of them, to say nothing of being barely

able to stand yourself. In such despair, degradation, and constant confusion of both matter and time, of flux and moving objects, I can hardly imagine finding anything worthy of serious pursuit, much less anything of value.

Instead, it is my duty to console myself, while I wait with patience for my natural death, in these principles only: one, that nothing will happen to me that is not in harmony with the nature of the universe; and the other, that it is in my own power never to act against my God and inner spirit; for there is no one who can force me to do wrong.

———◆———

THE WAY OF CONTEMPLATION

Learn the contemplative way of seeing how all things change into another, and immerse yourself in this; exercise mentally on this part of philosophy. For nothing else is as useful in producing greatness of spirit.

A man who thinks like this has already discounted the body, and since he knows that he must at some time—and who knows how soon?—withdraw from society and leave everything here, he devotes himself entirely to justice, and in all of life's events he resigns himself to universal Nature.

Now he wastes no time considering what anyone says, thinks, or does against him, finding himself content with just these two things: with acting justly in every moment, and being content with his own destiny; and discarding all distracting or busy pursuits, desiring nothing more than to follow the straight path of the law, and, by following it, to follow God.

———— ◆ ————

A SMALL ROLE

Think of the whole of being, of which you have a pittance; and the totality of time, of which a small measure has been set for you; and of everything that is arranged by destiny, and how tiny your role in it.

———•———

MELTING FLESH

From the universal substance, as if it were wax, Nature molds a horse, and when this has melted, it uses the matter to make a tree, then a man, and then something else; and each of these things lives for a very brief time.

But it is no more painful for a candle to melt, than there was pain in its creation.

———•———

ETERNAL FLUX

All particles of matter soon disintegrate into the substance of the whole; and every form or cause integrates into the primordial; and the memory of all things is swiftly overwhelmed in eternity.

———— ✦ ————

THE PHILOSOPHER'S
HALL OF FAME

The man itching for immortal fame does not see that everyone who remembers him will themselves soon die, and the next generation in its turn, until these memories, transmitted by men who foolishly admire and then die, will perish.

But even if these men were immortal and your memory stayed alive forever, what does it matter to you? What good is praise to the buried, or even the living, except for some practical use?

You reject Nature's gift today if you cling to what men may say of you tomorrow.

ALL THINGS HOLD
ALL THINGS

Anyone who has seen the present day has seen it all, both everything that has taken place since time began and everything that will be for all eternity; for all things are of one kind and one form.

DISSATISFACTION

Enough of this miserable life and its grumbling and restraints.

Why are you so disturbed? What's unsettling

you? What's new about it? Is it the appearance of something? Look clearly at it. Or is it the substance? Then face that. Because besides form and matter there is nothing else.

Even this late hour may be the right time for you to become a simpler and better person in the sight of the gods.

And remember, these things will remain the same whether we contemplate them for three years or a hundred.

Saving Your Life

Just consider, my friend, whether a pure spirit and virtue are anything other than saving your life and being saved.

Perhaps we need to discard the idea of longevity and cease loving this life, instead committing these things to God and, believing that no one ever escapes destiny, to consider, with that in mind, how we may live the best possible life in the time that remains.

❖ 7 ❖

AT ONE
WITH
NATURE

❋

THE WEB OF TIME

Whatever life brings you was prepared from all eternity; and the thread of causes was from the beginning of time spinning the fabric of your existence, and of every incidental fiber that weaves your web.

———————

PERSPECTIVE

Gaze in wonder at the ever-circling stars, as if you were floating among them; and consider the alterations of the elements, constantly changing one into another.

Thinking such thoughts you wash away the dust of life on earth.

———————

LIVING IN NATURE

If you don't know how the universe works, or what is happening in it, then you are alien to it; a fugitive, self-banished from the reasonable law of society; a blind man who has shut the eye of the mind, a beggar who needs other people to live off, and doesn't have the tools within that are needed for life.

To withdraw and separate yourself from the nature we all share because you are unhappy at your fate or destiny is to become a cancer on the Universe. For the same Nature that creates these events has also created you.

A man cut off from the community tears his own soul away from the universal soul, which is one.

———— •• ————

A REASON FOR EVERYTHING

Universal Nature felt an impulse to create the universe.

And now everything that comes into being follows as a necessary consequence. If this wasn't so, then even the main purpose that the ruling power of the Universe directs its own impulse toward would be lacking in reason.

To remember this helps you face uncertainty with tranquillity.

———— • ————

THE NATURAL LAW

If the ability to think is the heritage of humanity, then Reason, which makes us rational beings, and tells us what to do and what to avoid, must also be universal.

And if this is so, there must be a world law, and we are all fellow citizens of a political community. So the world has in some way a natural government that we all partake of. Where else can our capacity for law, reason, and thinking come from?

Just as my body is made up of a certain amount of earth, and my liquid elements from water, and whatever is hot and fiery in me from another form of heat. Nothing comes out from nothingness, just as nothing eventually returns to nonexistence; so also my thinking ability must come from some source.

ACCORDANCE

To a thinking being, an act that accords with Nature also accords with Reason.

THE RATIONAL UNIVERSE

In the unfolding of the sequence of created things, those that follow always fit perfectly with those that have preceded; for this sequence is not just a list of separate events tied together by necessity, but has a rational continuity.

Since all created things are joined together in harmony, so all phenomena coming into existence show not just succession but a wonderful organic connection.

———— • ————

THE LIVING UNIVERSE

Constantly regard the universe as a single living, being having one substance and one soul; observe how all creation relates to the cosmic consciousness of this one living being.

Observe too how everything moves with its impulse, working together to create all events, continuously spinning its delicate thread in the amazing complexity of its web.

———— • ————

ONLY ONE NATURE

Every single thing in life is fulfilled by following the nature of the Universe, for such fulfillment can't be found by following any rivals to Nature, either a nature that contains her from outside, or a nature contained within her, or even a nature outside and independent of her.

———— • ————

A STRANGE BEAUTY

A person with a feeling for Nature and deep insight into her creations finds a strange beauty even in her accidental displays.

Bread, for instance, when being baked, breaks open on the surface. Now these cracks, which are not intended by the baker, somehow catch the eye and stimulate our appetite for the food. Figs, too, gape open when they are ready, and in ripe olives their very nearness to decay adds a peculiar beauty to the fruit.

Ears of corn bending down, a lion's wrinkled brow, the foam that flows from a wild boar's mouth—you can't really call these beautiful, but because they follow the workings of Nature they lend a certain fascination and adornment to the whole.

Such a person will view the gaping jaws of real lions and tigers with more pleasure than the drawing and sculptures of artists. He will appreciate the mature grace of the old and see with innocent eyes the seductive bloom of the young.

Not everyone can see these things; only those who have cultivated a real intimacy with Nature and her works.

A Dialogue
with Nature

To Nature, who gives and takes back everything, the cultivated and modest person says, "Give us what you can; take back what you must." And this is said without pride, but in goodwill and obedience.

Going with
the Flow

Everything that flows from the gods is full of divine Nature. Our fate and fortune are not separate from Nature's creations, since they weave and link with the things made by Providence. Providence is the source from which all things flow; and allied to it is necessity, and the welfare of the entire universe.

As a part of the universe, you are also subject to whatever process is good for, and helps to maintain, the well-being of Nature.

Paradoxically, the universe is preserved by constant change. Not just by changes in the basic elements, but also by changes in things compounded from these elements.

Let these principles be enough for you to live by, and let them always be your guide. Lose your thirst for books so you don't die cursing your life, but cheerfully, truly, and from your heart be thankful to the gods.

BEYOND PLEASURE

Everything—a horse, a vine—exists for some purpose. Why are you surprised at this? The Sun God will say, "I am made for a purpose," and the rest of the gods will say the same. So what's your purpose in living? For pleasure? See if common sense accepts this idea.

TRUE BEAUTY

Anything that is beautiful is beautiful just as it is.

Praise forms no part of its beauty, since praise makes things neither better nor worse. This applies even more to what is commonly called beautiful: natural objects, for example, or works of art.

True beauty has no need of anything beyond itself.

In the same way the natural law, truth, compassion and modesty are not adorned by praise or spoiled by blame. Does the emerald lose its beauty because it is not admired? And what of gold, ivory, purple? Or a lute, a dagger, a rose?

TIMELY NATURE

Not only does Nature produce good things for all creatures, it also delivers them at just the right time.

IN PERSPECTIVE

In the vastness of the universe, Asia and Europe are just two small corners, all the seas are a single raindrop, and Mount Athos is a little clod; all of present time is but a pinpoint in eternity.

All things are petty, changeable, and perishable. And all things come from beyond, from that universal ruling principle, either directly or as a secondary consequence.

So the lion's gaping jaws, arsenic, and every other harmful thing, even down to thorns or a bog, are just by-products of this great and beautiful principle.

Don't imagine, then, that they're alien to the things you admire, but reflect upon the common source of all things.

———◆———

In Control

Does another man do me wrong? Let him worry about that. He has his own temperament and his own way of acting. As for me, I have only what universal Nature wills me to have; I do what my own nature wills me to do.

Producing
the Goods

One type of man, when he's done you a good turn, is ready to chalk it up to his own account as a favor expecting a return. Another doesn't go this far, but still in his own mind he sees you as his debtor and thinks you owe him. A third is not even conscious of what he's done, for he's like a vine that produces grapes and seeks no credit for producing its proper fruit.

Like a horse that has run his race, a hound when he has tracked game, or a bee when it has made honey, so when you have performed a good act, do not call out for witnesses but go on to do another, as a vine goes on to produce yet more grapes in season.

———•———

APT EXPERIENCE

Nothing happens to a person that is not a human possibility, just as an ox only experiences events suitable for the nature of an ox, and a vine those of the nature of a vine, and a stone what is proper for a stone.

So if all things experience what is both customary and natural, why should you complain? For Nature does not bring you anything you can't endure.

———•———

THE IMPARTIALITY
OF NATURE

Whoever acts unjustly violates creation. Since Nature has made rational creatures for each other's welfare and to help one another according to their merit, but not to injure each other, the person who opposes the will of creation is clearly guilty of violating this highest power.

Our universal Nature is the Nature that pervades all existence; and everything that now exists has a kinship to all other things that will come into existence. This universal Nature is called truth and is the original creator of all truths.

In the same way the person who intentionally lies is also guilty of opposing creation, since by deception he acts unfairly. And even if someone lies unintentionally, they are still at odds with universal Nature and disturb the natural order by fighting it: Nature has given us the ability to discern truth from lies, so when we deliberately neglect or subvert this ability, and think or act contrary to the truth, we are fighting against Nature, truth, and ourselves as well.

Similarly, any person who pursues pleasure as good, and avoids pain as evil, is guilty of contempt. This always leads to complaints that creation is unfair in rewarding bad and good inversely to their merits, because bad people often have a life full of the enjoyment of pleasures and acquire goods to provide it, while pains, troubles, and the events that cause them are often the lot of good people. A person who fears pain may also be afraid of what the future may bring, and this too is an error, while the one who fervently pursues pleasure will not stop at acts of injustice, and this is plainly a crime.

Those who wish to follow Nature and be in harmony with her must act as she acts, becoming indifferent to the same things that she treats without distinction—for Nature would not have created both pain and pleasure unless she was equally indifferent to both. Therefore whoever does not view with equanimity pain and pleasure, or death and life, or fame and dishonor, which universal Nature treats equally and impartially, is clearly acting against Nature.

———•———

THE FRUIT
OF REASON

God, the Universe, and humanity all produce fruit at the appropriate season. That our normal use of the phrase refers to vines and trees means nothing.

Reason, too, produces fruit both for itself and for the One, and from that process comes a multitude of other good things that share the quality of Reason itself.

———•———

THE POWER

Every instrument, tool, or utensil is good if it does the job it was designed for. Yet whoever made it is not present in the object.

But with things created by Nature, the power that made them is right there within them, and remains. Therefore it's right to worship this power, and to realize that if you live and act according to its will, everything in you will be in harmony with its energy.

Just as in the universe as a whole, all things in Nature are in unity with this power.

———✦———

THE CAUSES OF DESTINY

Just as we say, "The doctor prescribed for this man horseback riding, or cold baths, or walking barefoot," so we can also say, "The nature of the

universe prescribed for this man cancer or blind-
ness, or some other loss." With doctors, prescrip-
tion means to give a regime to create health; and
in the second case it means that everything that
happens to us is arranged in the right way according to destiny.

This is what we mean when we say that
things are suitable for us. It's what masons mean
when they say of the dressed stones in walls or
pyramids that they're suitable, that they fit perfectly one to another in a definite structure. For in
all of life there exists a similar fitness or harmony.

As the universe is a body composed of all the
bodies that exist, so destiny is formed from all the
causes that exist. And even the completely ignorant
understand what I mean, for they say, "Destiny
brought this to so and so." This result was delivered
and this was prescribed for him. Accordingly let us
accept these events, as well as the medicine the doctor prescribes. Many of the prescriptions will be
unpleasant, but we accept them in the hope of
health. Let the birth and growth of everything in the
world, which common nature judges to be good, be

judged by you in the same way as you look on your health. And so accept everything that happens, even if it seems unpleasant, because it leads to the health of the world and to the prosperity and happiness of the universe.

For the universe would not have created as many things as it has, if it weren't useful for the whole. Nature does not cause anything to happen to a creature that is not suitable for it. For two reasons then it is right to be content with what transpires: the one because it was done for you and prescribed for you, as part of the earliest causes spun with your destiny; and the other, because even simple things that happen to you can be a cause of happiness and perfection, even of the very continuance of the power that administers the universe.

If you separate anything from the connection and continuity of either the parts or the causes, you disturb the integrity of the whole. And when you are dissatisfied with life, you disconnect yourself, and this causes, as far as it is in your power, breakage and disruption.

THE VALUE OF
THE HEART

Empty ritual; stage plays; flocks of sheep; herds of cattle; military exercises; a bone thrown to the dogs; bits of bread tossed into fishponds; the burdens of worker ants; the scattering of scared mice; puppets pulled on a string—all of life.

You must stand kindly in the midst of all this and not be proud, yet understand that every man is worth just as much as the value of the things he's set his heart upon.

THE RIGHT SEASON

When any action stops at the right time, no harm is caused because it has ceased; and the person whose activity it was is no worse off because the action has ended.

Similarly, if life itself, which is the totality of all our acts, ceases at the right season, it experiences no harm because it's ended; and the person who has finished a series of acts at the right time has not suffered.

But the choice of season and the limits of time are set by Nature—sometimes, as in old age, our individual human nature, but always the same universal Nature; for it is by the continuous transformation of her parts that the whole world continues to be reborn ever young and perfect.

Now everything that is favorable to the whole is always good and in season. And so the fading away of life can't be evil, and, since it's both out of our control and totally selfless, it's not degrading either, but in fact is good, since it's timely, beneficial, and at one with the universal. So by moving on the right path and following the right way in our minds, we can be carried along on the same course as God.

A WORK OF NATURE

"When a mother kisses her child," said Epictetus, "she should whisper to herself, Tomorrow you might be dead."

"Ominous words," they told him.

"No word is ominous," said Epictetus, "that expresses a work of Nature. If this is the truth, it is also ominous to speak of the gathering of the corn."

———⋅✦⋅———

❖ 8 ❖

PEACE IS
IN YOUR
HANDS

❋

Contentment

If you can work sincerely and correctly on what is at hand, and do so with energy and calm, not allowing distractions, but keeping your inner spirit pure, as if you had only borrowed it and had to return it intact; if you can act in this way, hoping for nothing, fearing nothing, but satisfied with modulating your actions to the way of Nature, and with fearless truth in every word you utter, you will live contentedly.

And no one can take that from you.

———— ·•· ————

Return

When you are disturbed by events and lose your serenity, quickly return to yourself and don't stay upset longer than the experience lasts; for you'll have more mastery over your inner harmony by continually returning to it.

———— ·•· ————

MY TRUE HOME

You can live your life in harmony if you can take the right path, and think and act in the correct way.

These two things are shared both by the soul of God and the human soul, and so extend to the soul of every rational creature, not to be obstructed by another.

For I consider the good to be the dispensation of justice, and in its practice my desire can find its true home.

PAINFUL OPINION

Take away the belief "I have been harmed," and the hurt will disappear. Take away that sense of hurt, and the harm itself is gone.

AVOIDING ANXIETY

Don't let the future cause you anxiety, for the future will arrive in its own good time, and you'll have the same mind that you use now to deal with the present.

———•———

QUIET CONTEMPLATION

Moment by moment be mindful as a Roman and a man to deal with everything you have in hand with perfect and simple dignity; maintain a feeling of compassion, independence, and justice, and keep your mind free from all other thoughts.

If you could perform every action as if it were your last, dismissing all negligent thoughts and emotional reflexes from the rule of Reason, avoiding hypocrisy, selfishness, and bitterness, then you would free yourself, and lose any discontent with the life that has been given you.

You know how few things you really need to master to live a life that flows in quiet contemplation.

For the gods will demand nothing more from you if you live like this.

———— • ————

PAYING ATTENTION

Look deeply. Don't miss the inherent quality and value of everything.

———— • ————

WORK

Love the job you have learned, as poor as it may be, and find contentment in it. Spend the rest of your days like one who has committed his entire being to the gods, and so can be no one's tyrant or slave.

———— • ————

SIMPLIFYING YOUR LIFE

The philosopher Democritus said, "If you want to be content, do less." But it might be better to say, "Do only what is essential, and do the things that human reason alone demands, when it is needed." This brings the contentment of doing fewer things but doing them well.

Since most of what we say and do is completely redundant, if you follow this way, you will have more time and less trouble. So on every occasion ask yourself, "Is this really necessary?"

And remove not only unnecessary acts but the thoughts that precede them, for without excessive thoughts there would be no superfluous acts.

———— ✦ ————

STAYING CLOSE
TO THE CENTER

Don't act reluctantly, selfishly, inconsiderately, or distractedly. Don't let your thoughts be altered by overrefinement and pretensions, and avoid being a windbag and a busybody.

Just let the spirit that dwells inside you be the guardian of a true mature man, a statesman, a Roman, and a ruler, who has taken his position like a soldier waiting for the Retreat to sound, ready to leave this life; a man whose beliefs don't need to be sworn to by himself or confirmed by anyone else.

Why not be happy, since you need no outside source to help you, nor to seek tranquillity from anyone else?

You should stand up by yourself, not be held up by others.

THE MIRACLE

If you can find qualities in life better than justice, truth, self-control, and courage, or anything finer than your own mind's contentment in harmonizing your actions to the rule of Reason and satisfaction with your own destiny; if you can find anything greater than these qualities, turn to it with all your heart, and enjoy the miracle you have found.

But if nothing seems to be better than the spirit within you that contains all your desires, and has carefully sifted all your thoughts and impressions and, as Socrates says, detached itself from the world of sensuality, and bowed to the gods and given you compassion toward mankind; if you find everything else worthless and pettier than this spirit, then there is no need to look for anything else.

Because if you just once turn and falter, you will remove yourself from that true good you already possess. It's a tragedy to allow other ambitions, like fame, or power, wealth, or pleasure, to compete with what you know is rationally and practically good. Though you think you can keep these ambitions in control, you will soon find that they have taken over and carried you away.

So it's better to simply and in perfect freedom choose the better way and stick to it.

———◆———

ORDINARY LIFE

Everything that happens is as ordinary and obvious as a rose in spring or a peach in summer; and the same is true for disease and death, slander and intrigue, and everything else that bothers or delights fools.

———◆———

CHERISHING IN
MODERATION

Don't worry about what you don't have, but think instead about what you do possess.

Of these blessings, select the best, and consider how eagerly you would want them if they were not already yours.

At the same time take care that your pleasure in possession doesn't cause you to cherish them too dearly, since their loss would disturb your peace of mind.

———◆———

THE STRENGTH
OF WISDOM

Nothing can happen to you that Nature has not prepared you to bear. The same events may happen to your neighbor, but he stays firm and remains unharmed; either by ignoring the experience, or because he can show a greatness of spirit.

Isn't it a shame that ignorance and vanity should be stronger than wisdom?

———— • ————

FORTUNATE

Be like the cliff continually battered by the waves that stands firm and tames the fury of the water.

"I'm miserable, because this has happened to me."

No. Say instead, "I am content even though this has happened, because I remain free from distress, neither crushed by the present nor afraid of the future."

For this might have happened to anyone; but not everyone would have remained free from bitterness. So why say this is misfortune rather than good fortune?

Can you call anything a misfortune, if it is not

contrary to human nature, or contrary to the will of human nature? You know the will of Nature. Why let what has happened prevent you from being fair, generous, self-controlled, mindful, and firm against slander and lies? Will it prevent you from having modesty, freedom, and everything else that enables human nature to be fulfilled?

Remember on every occasion that annoys you to apply this principle: this is not a misfortune; to bear it bravely is good fortune.

TRUE FREEDOM

The way you intend to live after death can also be practiced here on earth. If men stop you, then leave this life now, without expressing anger at fate.

"The house is full of smoke, so I'm getting out now."

Why do you think this is a big deal?

So long as nothing like this drives me out, I

remain, am free, and no one shall stop me from doing what I choose—and I choose to live in harmony with my nature: that of a rational and social animal.

———•———

SETTING YOUR
MIND FREE

Let your guiding part, your mind, be untroubled by impulses of the flesh, whether of pleasure or of pain. Don't let your mind join with them, but let it spiral itself in and limit those stirrings to the flesh itself.

But when these impulses rise up to the mind because of the union that naturally exists in a mind and body that is one, then don't strive to resist the feeling, because it's natural.

What's not natural is your mind adding a good or bad judgment to the sensation.

———•———

TRUE FREEDOM IS MIND

Meditate on the true nature of things stripped of their covering; the aims of action. Consider the nature of pain and pleasure, death and fame; how each person causes their own suffering; how no one is restricted by their neighbors; that true freedom is in the mind.

———•———

THE OBJECTS OF LOVE

Love only what happens to you and is destined for you. What could be more suitable than that?

———•———

THE PRINCIPLE
AT WORK

Withdraw into your inner self. The rational principle that rules there is content with itself when it acts justly, and so maintains its own tranquillity.

———•———

KEEPING TRANQUILLITY

It's in your power to live without restraint and in the serenest state of mind, even if all men shout out against you; even if wild beasts tear to pieces this dense body that has grown around you.

In the midst of all this, what is it that stops the mind from keeping itself in tranquillity?

In true judgment of all that surrounds it, the mind can say to anything that falls under its gaze, "This is what you are in substance, in reality, even though men's opinions may give you another appearance."

And in an elegant use of the objects presented to it, the mind says to whatever it finds at hand, "You are just the thing I was looking for."

To me the present itself is always material for rational and political virtue; for the exercise of the art of God or man. For all existence has a relationship either to God or humanity, and is neither novel nor hard to deal with, but familiar and easy to work on.

———— • ————

THE BENEFIT SYSTEM

No one tires of getting benefits, and to benefit another is to act according to Nature. Why then are you tired of the benefits you receive by giving them to others?

———— • ————

CLOSE TO PERFECTION

If your current opinions are founded on understanding, and your daily conduct is aimed at social good, and you have a feeling of contentment with everything that turns up, what more can you need?

———◆———

PROTECTING SACRED PRINCIPLES

Hatred, war, disorder, illness, and slavery will daily wipe out these sacred principles of yours. How many things do you imagine (and neglect) without studying their inmost nature?

It's your duty to examine every object and to perform every act so that, at one and the same time, the ability to deal with all practicalities is perfected, the contemplative mind is exercised, and the self-confidence that comes from clear knowledge of every relevant detail is maintained without showing off, but is not concealed.

Will you never find the happiness of pure simplicity or dignity? Or the serene understanding of the inner essence of each object? Both its form and the elements that compound it, what place it has in the universe, how long it can exist, who can possess it, who gives it, and who can take it away?

———————

IN TUNE WITH NATURE

If anyone despises me, that's their problem. My only concern is not doing or saying anything deserving of contempt.

Does anyone hate me? That's also their problem. But I will be gentle and compassionate toward everyone, ready to show them their errors, not reproachfully, and not by showing off my patience, but genuinely and honestly.

Your inner spirit should be like this, and you shouldn't be seen by the gods either discontented or complaining.

How can you harm yourself, if you are right now acting in tune with your own nature, and feel satisfied in every moment by Nature's great plan? You as a human being have been placed here to realize whatever blessings can be created for everyone's benefit.

———— • ————

CALM SAILING

Everything is what your judgment says it is, and that power is yours. When you choose to take away your opinion, you become like a sailor who has rounded the headland and finds a calm and tranquil bay.

———— • ————

ENDURANCE

All of life's events occur in such a way that your nature can either endure them, or it can't. So if events happen that you can bear, don't complain, but bear them as well as your nature allows.

But if something happens that your nature can't endure, you still mustn't complain, for that event will end, but only after it has finished you.

Remember, however, that you are created by Nature to endure anything that your own judgment declares bearable and tolerable, by thinking that it's either your duty or in your self-interest to do so.

———— ◆ ————

THE ROOT OF DISSATISFACTION

If you're bothered by something outside yourself, it's not the thing that's disturbing you, but your own judgment about it, and it's in your power to wipe this judgment out right now.

If it's something in your own character that disturbs you, who can stop you from cultivating better principles?

And it's the same if you're troubled because you're not doing something that you feel is right—why not act rather than complain?

"But a massive obstacle is in the way."

Then don't blame yourself, for the responsibility is not yours.

"I don't think it's worthwhile to live, if I can't put this right."

Then depart this life with the same satisfaction as a man who has fulfilled all his aims, gracefully accepting the very obstacles that oppose you.